Landscape
Conservation Law

Present Trends and
Perspectives in International and
Comparative Law

T0303191

Landscape Conservation Law

Present Trends and Perspectives in International and Comparative Law

P R O C E E D I N G S OF
A COLLOQUIUM

Commemorating the 50th Anniversary of
IUCN, The World Conservation Union
30 October 1998
Palais du Luxembourg
Paris

Environmental Policy and Law Paper No. 39

IUCN - The World Conservation Union
2000

Published by: IUCN, Gland, Switzerland and Cambridge, UK

                         IUCN Commission on Environmental Law
                         IUCN World Commission on Protected Areas
                         Société Française pour le Droit de l'Environnement

The World Conservation Union

Copyright: © 2000 International Union for Conservation of Nature and Natural Resources

                         Reproduction of this publication for educational or other non-commercial pur-
                         poses is authorised without prior permission from the copyright holder provided
                         the source is fully acknowledged.

                         Reproduction of this publication for resale or other commercial purposes is
                         prohibited without prior written permission of the copyright holder.

Citation: IUCN Commission on Environmental Law, (2000). *Landscape Conservation
                         Law: Present Trends and Perspectives in International and Comparative Law.*
                         IUCN, Gland, Switzerland and Cambridge, UK. viii + 102 p.

ISBN: 2-8317-0528-2

Cover design by: IUCN Environmental Law Centre

Cover photo: "Peintre en Forêt" by Jules Coignet, Museum Auberge Ganne in Barbizon.
                         Courtesy of: Éditions Gaud - 11, rue Brulard - 77950 Moisenay - France

Layout by: Barbara Weiner, Desktop Publications Co-ordinator

Printed by: Daemisch Mohr, Siegburg, Germany

Available from: IUCN Publications Services Unit
                         219c Huntingdon Road, Cambridge, CB3 0DL, UK
                         or
                         IUCN Environmental Law Centre
                         Godesberger Allee 108-112, D-53175 Bonn, Germany
                         A catalogue of IUCN publications is also available

Table of Contents

Foreword

The Colloquium on Landscape Conservation Law – Present Trends and Perspectives in International and Comparative Law took place in Paris on 30 October 1998.

It was convened a few days before the ceremonies commemorating the 50th anniversary of IUCN – The World Conservation Union which took place in Fontainebleau, where IUCN was created in 1948. It was part of a number of similar events which took place around the world on that occasion.

Two Commissions of IUCN took this initiative: the World Commission on Protected Areas and the Commission on Environmental Law. They joined forces with a member of IUCN in France – the Société Française pour le Droit de l'Environnement (SFDE) – which, in addition to its substantive contribution to the Colloquium, organised and steered its preparation. The Fondation d'entreprise Gaz de France generously contributed to its success by providing logistical and financial support.

The attention given to landscape in environmental law is new and the subject raises a series of interesting problems, which have been highlighted at the Colloquium. Its central theme was the draft European Landscape Convention prepared by the Council of Europe, which is the first of its kind. Since the Colloquium took place, the draft has evolved, and has reached its almost final form – it is expected to be adopted during 2000. This is the reason why, in Annex 1 to these proceedings, we reproduce both the version available at the time of the Colloquium, and the current draft.

After reviewing this draft Convention, the Colloquium was of the view that there was a need for close coordination between the final text of the Convention and a parallel area of technical and policy work: Action theme 4 (Landscape) of the Pan European Biological and Landscape Diversity Strategy. After the meeting, therefore, we wrote to the Council of Europe to that effect, and offered our continuing assistance in the finalisation of the Convention.

Another aspect of the Colloquium was to explore the elements of landscape conservation law in various parts of the world. The participation of members of the Steering Committee of the IUCN Commission on Environmental Law allowed for the presentation of a variety of national and regional perspectives.

We are pleased to make the proceedings of the Colloquium available, and hope that they will inspire continued work on this important issue.

Finally, we would like to reiterate our thanks to the Société Française pour le Droit de l'Environnement, in particular to Jérôme Fromageau, President of its Section Île de France, for his tireless efforts in making this Colloquium a success. We are also much indebted to Elizabeth Delorme, Secretary General of the Fondation d'entreprise Gaz de France, for her personal commitment, and the support of the foundation.

Special thanks for the organisation of the colloquium go to Isabelle Trinquelle, Secretary of the Section Ile de France of the SFDE, and to Milena Bellini, CEL volunteer-consultant, who has transcribed and edited the colloquium proceedings.

Adrian Phillips
Chairman
IUCN World Commission on Protected Areas

Nicholas A. Robinson
Chairman
IUCN Commission on Environmental Law

March 2000

INTRODUCTION

Session chaired by Nicholas A. Robinson, Chairman, IUCN Commission on Environmental Law; Professor of Law, Pace University School of Law, N.Y., USA

Introductory Remarks by the Chairman

On behalf of the Commission on Environmental Law (CEL), it is my profound honour to welcome you to this colloquium commemorating the 50th anniversary of the founding of the International Union for the Conservation of Nature and Natural Resources – a founding that took place in the *République Française*. It is entirely fitting that we commemorate our 50th anniversary in Paris, as it was here that, in 1948, the Swiss League for the Protection of Nature, a non-governmental organisation now called Pro Natura, joined forces with UNESCO and the Government of France to establish a new union for the conservation of nature.

We are very honoured that the French Senate has permitted us to hold this meeting here in the *Salle Médicis*. It is a great honour and quite appropriate for CEL to have a Parliament for a setting, because, as do Parliaments all around the world, CEL works for the development of law.

Under the able leadership of Dr. Wolfgang Burhenne, IUCN has done much to realise the vision of developing an international law for the environment. He was key to the development of the Convention on International Trade in Endangered Species of Wild Flora and Fauna,[1] which gave us new tools to fight against the extinction of species. In 1992 IUCN was instrumental in the development of the Convention on Biological Diversity[2] under the expert leadership of Françoise Burhenne-Guilmin.

Many others have taken up this task of developing International Environmental Law. The Draft European Landscape Convention, developed by the Council of Europe, which we shall examine in this symposium, is a most valuable contribution to the development of the law for nature and culture, as we will see throughout the day. The International Council of Environmental Law, of which Dr. Burhenne is Executive Governor, and IUCN, under the able leadership of Dr. Parvez Hassan, the former Chair of the Commission on Environmental Law, have developed the International Covenant on Environment and Development, a draft international agreement which holds great promise. It was launched during the United Nations General Assembly's Congress on Public International Law, held in New York in 1995, to commemorate the 50th anniversary of the United Nations. Although IUCN and others have done much to develop environmental law, ours is a very young discipline and we have much more to achieve.

IUCN is not the only organisation contributing to the development of environmental law, I wish to pay tribute to the *Société Française pour le Droit de l'Environnement* (SFDE), It has done a great deal to advance environmental law, not just in France, but also internationally. One of its leaders and a principal drafter of the Draft European Convention on Landscape is the member of CEL, Prof. Michel Prieur, who, unfortunately, could not be with us today. Prof. Michel Prieur was the first Chief Editor of the *Revue Juridique de l'Environnement*, which is published under the patronage of the SFDE. I was so excited when the SFDE was founded and started this publication, that I subscribed to it immediately and on the occasion of the SFDE and IUCN's co-sponsorship of this colloquium, I brought with me the first edition of the *Revue*.

I also wish to thank the Section Ile de France of the SFDE, particularly Professor Jérôme Fromageau, for the excellent leadership in the organisation of this colloquium; all of us in IUCN are honoured to be associated with the SFDE. May I also thank the IUCN World Commission on Protected Areas and its Chairman, Adrian Phillips, who will be giving a welcome address shortly. The cooperation between the Experts Commissions of IUCN is one of the strongest links in the chain for the conservation of nature that was forged in France 50 years ago.

---

[1] CITES, Washington, 3 March 1973, 993 UNTS 243.

[2] Convention on Biological Diversity, Rio de Janeiro, 5 June 1992, 32 ILM 822, 1992.

A special word of thanks goes to the *Gaz de France Foundation*. Even before I knew the *Société Française pour le Droit de l'Environnement*, I knew *Gaz de France*. You may wonder why someone from New York would know *Gaz de France*. Well, if you are someone who is camping, backpacking, going into the wild, into the mountains, you must carry a small cooking stove with you, and if you carry a small cooking stove, you will know the small blue canisters that *Gaz de France* manufactures and sells around the world. I have been carrying *Gaz de France* on my back into the mountains of Alaska, the Rocky Mountains of Canada and the United States, the Sierra Nevada Mountains of California, the Adirondack Mountains of New York State and I am much in debt to the ingenuity of *Gaz de France*. It is a special pleasure for me to thank *Gaz de France* for making interpretation available today and for the reception they will host for this 50th anniversary colloquium.

Finally a word of thanks, in advance, to the interpreters, who simultaneously translate our presentations in French and English. We are much in debt to them for the contribution that their interpretation will make to better communication in this international gathering, aimed at furthering the protection of our cultural and natural environment.

I am confident that this colloquium will greatly contribute to advance the law of the environment and set the agenda for the next 50 years of environmental law development in IUCN. I thank all of you who have taken the time to join us today to participate in what promises to be an interesting and active discussion.

Adrian Phillips, *Chair, IUCN World Commission on Protected Areas; former Director General of the Countryside Commission of England and Wales; Professor, Cardiff University, UK*

In my capacity as Chair of the World Commission on Protected Areas, it is with great pleasure that I speak immediately after my friend and colleague, Nick Robinson, on the occasion of this important colloquium on landscape and law. The World Commission on Protected Areas (WCPA), one of IUCN's six Commissions, is the global network of experts working in this field. It is comprised of some 1300 experts from around the world, working in a volunteer capacity. Our mission is to promote the cause of protected areas, parks, reserves, and so forth, in the belief that such areas are essential for the conservation of biodiversity and, indeed, for human wellbeing and development.

Long before words like biodiversity and sustainable development were known, the concept of landscape was a driving force behind the creation of protected areas. Indeed, ever since the start of the protected areas movement in 1872 in the United States with the Yellowstone Park, the beauty and richness of landscape has moved people and countries to set aside special areas and give them a particular degree of protection. Indeed, IUCN specifically recognises one type of protected area, the so-called "Category V", as areas for landscape protection. Such areas are especially important in Europe but, increasingly, I believe that landscape protection is seen as relevant to the conservation and sustainable development needs of other regions, including developing regions.

So when Nick Robinson invited me to associate WCPA with this event, convened as a contribution to the celebration of IUCN's 50th anniversary, I was delighted, as it provides an opportunity to build on and to internationalise the cooperation, which the two Commissions have already developed, in the work on the Draft European Landscape Convention.

The Programme has been well designed for this purpose, bringing together, from around the world, the experiences of legal and protected area experts in working on the interface between landscape and law. In a paper on the Draft European Landscape Convention, which I shall present later this morning, I hope to show why this is potentially such a profitable area for cooperation.

Finally, I would like to say how much WCPA also recognises and appreciates the help given by the SFDE, particularly Professor Jérôme Fromageau, in co-sponsoring and organising this colloquium. I join Nick in paying generous tribute to the support given by the *Gaz de France* Foundation. I am certain that their support for this event will be amply rewarded by a stimulating and instructive day.

Jérôme Fromageau, *Président, Section Île de France, Société Française pour le Droit de l'Environnement; vice-doyen, Faculté Jean Monnet, Université de Paris Sud; membre de la Commission du droit de l'environnement de l'UICN*

Je voudrais m'associer aux remerciements qui ont été adressés à l'instant, remercier donc tout particulièrement les Sénateurs François Bleziot et Philippe Richert, qui nous ont permis de nous rencontrer ici, pour cette journée de réflexion sur le paysage à la fois dans le cadre du droit international, mais aussi du droit comparé. Je voudrais exprimer aussi notre gratitude à la *Fondation d'entreprise Gaz de France* représentée par Elisabeth Delorme, sa Secrétaire générale, dont l'appui a été remarquablement efficace. Comme le président vous l'a dit tout à l'heure, la *Fondation d'entreprise Gaz de France* s'est investie dans des domaines directement liés à la gestion des paysages Elle a mené des opérations remarquables telles que la réhabilitation des chemins de randonnée qui sont, d'ailleurs, réellement bien appropriés pour mieux comprendre le paysage et pour mieux l'apprécier. Elle a participé à la restauration d'un certain nombre de sites, tout à fait emblématiques, notamment à la Pointe du Raz, dans le département du Finistère, où le travail accompli en collaboration avec les collectivités territoriales est, à bien des égards, exemplaire, mais aussi au Cirque de Gavarnie, dans les Pyrénées, intégré au Mont Perdu, inscrit récemment sur la liste du patrimoine mondial de l'humanité.

Ce colloque est consacré au droit du paysage en droit international et en droit comparé, sujet audacieux, s'il en est un. Laissons de côté, pour l'instant, la définition même du terme de paysage sur laquelle nous reviendrons à propos du projet de Convention sur le paysage. Le titre du colloque laisse entendre que le paysage serait un objet de droit, un objet de droit autonome, ce qui n'est pas, bien sûr, évident. Quand on parle d'objet de droit autonome, pour ce qui concerne le paysage, c'est essentiellement par rapport au droit de l'environnement et au droit de l'urbanisme. Le paysage est effectivement un élément de l'environnement au sens large du terme, il n'est pas uniquement lié à la nature, mais il est indissociable de l'environnement, il est l'oeuvre, sans fin, de l'homme et de la nature. Vouloir le détacher, par souci d'efficacité, du droit de l'environnement, risque de faire perdre tout le terrain qui a été progressivement conquis depuis un vingtaine d'années et qui a consisté à intégrer petit à petit le paysage dans tous les domaines qui relèvent de ce qu'il est convenu d'appeler le droit de l'urbanisme et le droit de l'environnement.

Le paysage n'est pas qualifié juridiquement, mais l'absence d'une telle qualification ne saurait être un obstacle à la mise en oeuvre d'une politique du paysage, à condition, bien sûr, de disposer d'instruments efficaces pour protéger les éléments individuels qui le composent. Le paysage et l'environnement définissent un patrimoine collectif, un patrimoine commun, même s'il y a une différence entre ces deux termes.

L'environnement peut être analysé, décomposé par secteurs qui présentent chacun leur spécificité d'analyse et de gestion. Le paysage, par contre, évoque une approche unitaire, un ensemble composé de signes qui définissent, précisément, une structure unitaire. Autrement dit, le paysage est une manière, bien singulière, de concevoir l'environnement puisqu'il implique une évaluation qualitative de l'environnement, qui prend en compte l'évolution et l'adaptation d'usages au nouveau système de production.

C'est pourquoi il apparaît plus aisé d'individualiser ce qu'il ne faut pas faire, que de savoir ce qui peut être fait dans un paysage. Par exemple, là où le paysage est le résultat d'une stratification historique qui le caractérise de manière systématique, dans toute son unité, les transformations sont souvent très faibles par rapport aux caractères historiques qui eux demeurent forts. Dans ce cas, le problème est d'individualiser des éléments stables, autrement dit ceux qui constituent la référence invariable du paysage, qui relèvent de pratiques agricoles ancestrales, pour prendre l'exemple du paysage rural; et même si ces pratiques agricoles changent, ces éléments sont le signe qui structure fondamentalement le paysage.

Par ailleurs, il me semble qu'il faut récuser l'opposition artificielle entre une protection de la nature qui pourrait être strictement fondée sur la science, et qui serait complètement objective, et une conservation des paysages qui serait exclusivement culturelle et donc totalement sociale et subjective. Dans la politique de la protection de la nature, nos sociétés opèrent des choix de type social et culturel. Et si la politique de la protection de la nature est fondée sur des données scientifiques objectives, un choix est nécessairement opéré, elle n'est donc que partiellement objective. De même, dans le domaine du paysage, ce dernier est finalement le résultat d'un croisement entre des données objectives et le regard social qui est porté sur l'espace.

Par ailleurs, nous sommes en mesure de caractériser et de hiérarchiser les paysages, par conséquent de leur donner une valeur, et à partir de là de mener des actions de conservation, si bien que la question du paysage est beaucoup moins suggestive qu'il n'y paraît. Il peut y avoir une identification des objets paysagers à valeur reconnue, et d'ailleurs il est frappant de constater que certains archétypes du paysage sont universellement reconnus. C'est là déjà un point d'approche tout à fait intéressant pour envisager le paysage au niveau international.

Nous pouvons mener des politiques de paysage avec des fondements objectifs. Mais ces politiques de paysage doivent se distinguer, en partie tout au moins, et c'est là une des difficultés des politiques de protection de la nature. Il y a des recoupements, il y a aussi des oppositions. Une grande montagne, par exemple, pour laquelle on reconnaît une beauté universelle, peut en même temps, et c'est fréquent heureusement, receler des biotopes remarquables pour la faune, mais ce regroupement total des enjeux écologiques et des enjeux paysagers est loin d'être systématique. Au fond il y a une place pour les enjeux écologiques et puis il y a une place aussi pour des enjeux paysagers qui peuvent n'avoir, nous disent certains paysagistes, aucun rapport avec des enjeux écologiques dans des sites totalement artificialisés.

Le paysage n'est pas seulement une forme de représentation, une apparence, mais c'est aussi le résultat d'une composition entre la nature et la culture. C'est ce qui ressort bien, par exemple, dans la Convention pour la protection du patrimoine mondial,[3] avec cette dichotomie, d'un côté le patrimoine culturel, de l'autre le patrimoine naturel, et puis l'émergence depuis quelques années d'un patrimoine, si je puis dire, de transition: celui que caractérisent les "sites mixtes".

Du point de vue comparatif, nombreux sont les pays qui abordent la question du paysage par deux voix bien différenciées: d'une part, la voix politique des espaces protégés, c'est-à-dire les sites remarquables – c'est l'idée de la conservation, du maintien en l'état – et, d'autre part, celle de la prise en charge du paysage par des lois d'aménagement, d'urbanisme, de planification du territoire et de l'environnement. S'il convient donc de dégager le droit du paysage du droit de l'urbanisme, cela ne veut pas dire que dans le droit de l'urbanisme et de la planification il ne doit pas y avoir une dimension paysagère comme dans le droit de l'environnement.

Pour autant, il n'est pas certain que l'on puisse aller beaucoup plus loin dans la progression de ce droit du paysage qui nous semble, par ailleurs, si nécessaire. En réalité, les politiques nouvelles de protection et de gestion des paysages s'efforcent de combiner les préoccupations de protection du patrimoine, de l'environnement, de l'aménagement du territoire et de l'urbanisme. La question est de savoir quelle politique du paysage mener en dehors des sites protégés? C'est bien là,

---

[3]   World Heritage Convention, Paris, 16 November 1972, 1037 UNTS 151.

finalement, tout le problème pour ce qui concerne les débats les plus complexes autour du paysage. Quelle politique du paysage mener en dehors des sites protégés, qui ne représentent d'ailleurs qu'une très faible fraction du territoire européen? Face à cette question, les pouvoirs publics ont toujours été relativement muets, voire incapables de définir de véritables doctrines et en définitive, me semble-t-il, la seule doctrine qui se soit jusqu'à maintenant imposée est celle qui a été mise en oeuvre dans le domaine des ensembles urbains et des monuments historiques. Elle vaut ce qu'elle vaut, c'est la "doctrine de l'intégration", mais les observateurs les plus critiques diront aussi que c'est la "doctrine de la dissimulation" ou de la "simulation".

Traditionnellement donc, les textes n'ont pris en compte le paysage que dans la mesure où il représentait un intérêt artistique, légendaire, ou pittoresque. Cela a été le cas des premières législations européennes, par exemple la loi de 1906 pour le paysage en France. Ce sont ces lois qui ont incité les Etats, dès 1910, à oeuvrer et à réfléchir sur la question du paysage. On a pu parler, à juste titre, d'une politique élitiste, ségrégationniste, du paysage, ce dernier n'étant simplement considéré que comme un conservatoire sans avenir, qu'il convient de protéger, de sauvegarder de manière statique. Les paysages du quotidien, les paysages de l'ordinaire, ne sont pas concernés en tant que tels, et il est de toutes les façons évident qu'on ne peut pas étendre ce droit de l'exception à l'ensemble du territoire d'un pays, à l'ensemble du territoire d'un continent.

Pourtant, le "paysage du quotidien", qui ne fait pas l'objet d'une protection juridique spécifique, est un facteur d'identité en évolution permanente qui n'est plus ignoré par le droit: les systèmes juridiques envisagent soit des instruments diversifiés de protection généralisée, soit des mécanismes relevant du droit rural, du droit de l'environnement, du droit de l'urbanisme ou de l'aménagement.

Peut-être conviendrait-il, pour donner une valeur sociale renforcée au paysage et l'accompagner par un encadrement juridique plus efficace, de le valoriser en lui donnant un statut juridique de bien commun, ce que tente de proposer le projet de convention européenne du paysage, projet qui, d'une certaine manière, s'inscrit dans une longue histoire: celle de la protection du patrimoine culturel et naturel.

Françoise Burhenne-Guilmin, *Chef, Centre du droit de l'environnement de l'UICN*

Nous fêtons le 50e anniversaire de l'UICN, créée près d'ici, à Fontainebleau, en 1948, dans le but d'établir un dialogue entre gouvernements et organisations non-gouvernementales, un dialogue entre disciplines, un dialogue entre experts. L'UICN est une organisation composée d'Etats, plus de soixante-dix, d'agences gouvernementales et d'organismes de protection de la nature et de l'environnement du secteur privé. Des membres qui se retrouvent, sur un pied d'égalité, tous les trois ans, pour prendre ensemble des décisions sur la politique de l'Union. C'est donc une organisation assez particulière et disons le, assez encourageante. Mais l'UICN est aussi une organisation où l'expertise individuelle, groupée en commissions internationales, joue un grand rôle. Ce sont ces réseaux d'experts qui ont permis à l'UICN son premier essor et qui continuent, à mon avis, d'être une sève inépuisable.

Nous fêtons aussi le 35e, ou le 40e anniversaire, selon la date que vous voulez considérer, de ce qui est devenu le Programme du droit de l'environnement de l'UICN, qui a commencé très modestement par un comité temporaire en 1958, comité de volontaires, et qui est devenu une Commission de législation en 1963. Rappelez-vous: le mot environnement n'existait pas. Rappelez-vous: le droit jouait un rôle très modeste, et parfois même, au sein de l'UICN, un rôle très contesté. Qui en avait besoin? Bien qu'en fait, lors de leur réunion à Fontainebleau, les fondateurs de l'UICN aient tout de suite indiqué qu'un des buts de l'organisation devait être la conclusion d'un accord international sur la conservation de la nature, il a fallu vingt cinq ans pour commencer à le réaliser.[4]

Au cours de son existence le Programme du droit de l'environnement s'est voulu un précurseur dans plusieurs domaines. Dans un premier temps il s'est profilé dans le domaine de l'information. Même en débutant, dans les années soixante, nous n'avions pas devant nous une page blanche, différents droits, celui de l'eau par exemple, celui de la protection de la nature, étaient déjà développés, et donc dès les années soixante le programme a établi une banque de données qui est devenue le système d'information du droit de l'environnement de l'UICN. Trente ans plus tard, nous essayons de le mettre sur Internet, nous le partageons avec le Programme des Nations Unies pour l'Environnement et espérons pouvoir le mettre à la disposition de tous très bientôt.

En parallèle, le besoin de se doter d'une infrastructure juridique internationale s'est fait sentir très tôt. La Commission et le Centre, créé en 1970, s'engagent dans cette voie, commençant par un accord tripartite sur l'ours polaire.[5] Cette voie qui chemine pour arriver trente ans plus tard à la première grande convention sectorielle sur les espèces et les écosystèmes: la biodiversité. Entre temps, comme le Président vient de le dire, il y a eu la Convention de Washington sur le commerce des espèces,[6] la Convention sur les espèces migratrices[7] et des conventions régionales tout aussi importantes. Je pense que c'est dans ce domaine que l'UICN a eu, peut-être, les plus grands succès.

Mais l'évolution continue au rythme des besoins; l'accent se met sur les législations nationales, en particulier celles des pays en voie de développement. C'est pourquoi un programme a été créé en 1990: le service du droit de l'environnement, qui a pour but de répondre aux besoins de ces pays en matière de législations nationales de protection de l'environnement, adaptées à leur besoins spécifiques. Le défi ici est de trouver des solutions sur mesures, qui ne sont pas nécessairement celles qui se pratiquent dans les pays où le droit de l'environnement a vu le jour.

Cela signifie aussi s'engager dans la voie du développement durable et voir ce que cela veux dire du point de vue du droit de l'environnement. Qui dit développement durable, dit formation de ceux qui en sont les acteurs, en droit de l'environnement comme dans d'autres domaines. Voilà donc, trente ans plus tard, le dernier né des grands axes du Programme du droit de l'environnement de l'UICN: la formation des cadres enseignants. Pas plus tard qu'hier, le Comité directeur de notre Commission a décidé de mettre l'accent sur la création d'une Académie internationale du droit de l'environnement qui regrouperait des universités de toutes les parties du monde.

La conquête continue et le droit de l'environnement évolue. Je ne voudrais pas finir sans souligner les liens entre le Programme du droit de l'environnement de l'UICN et la Société française pour le droit de l'environnement. La contribution de plusieurs de ses membres au travail de l'UICN a été, et reste, importante. En particulier, voudrais-je mentionner Alex Kiss et Cyrille de Klemm, avec lesquels j'ai passé de nombreuses nuits blanches, discutant des textes de projets de convention. Je les remercie. Je me réjouis de fêter avec vous, au berceau de l'UICN, son 50e anniversaire.

---

[4] CITES, Washington, 3 March 1973, 993 UNTS 243. Agreement on the Conservation of Polar Bears, Oslo, 15 November 1973, 13 ILM 13, 1974.

[5] *Cf supra at N. 4.*

[6] *Cf supra at N. 4.*

[7] Convention on the Conservation of Migratory Species of Wild Animals, Bonn, 23 June 1979, 19 ILM 11, 1980.

PART I

INTERNATIONAL LAW

Session chaired by Dr. Wolfgang E. Burhenne, former Chair, IUCN Commission on Environmental Law; Executive Governor, International Council of Environmental Law

Introductory Remarks by the Chairman

I would like to start with a personal remark: I am very happy to be in the French Senate again. I have been here many times. Edgar Faure, the former President of the Senate, was the chairman of an international institute of which I was vice-chairman. That is how I had the opportunity to come here on several occasions. I thank the organisers, who have made it possible for this colloquium to take place here.

This session will consider international law on landscape conservation, in particular the Draft European Convention on this subject. The experts that will intervene during this session will present the draft Convention in detail but, at the outset, I would like to consider some background information on the history of the text we are dealing with.

Already in June 1997, the Congress of Local and Regional Authorities of Europe decided to organise a Conference in Florence. It took place in April 1998 and the first draft of what was to become the European Landscape Convention was discussed. In addition to officials from National Ministries, representatives of organisations such as the World Heritage Committee and the World Heritage Centre of the United Nations Educational, Scientific and Cultural Organisation (UNESCO), the European Commission and the Committee on Regions of the European Union participated. IUCN was present through its Commission on Environmental Law and the World Commission on Protected Areas. There was also quite a large number of representatives of non-governmental organisations.

In October 1998, the member of parliament Victor Ruffy (Switzerland) presented his first report on the subject to the Standing Committee of the Parliamentary Assembly of the Council of Europe. The discussion continued in the Assembly, which adopted Resolution 150 (1998). In compliance with the wishes of the Congress, the Resolution asked the Assembly to consider the Preliminary Draft European Landscape Convention set out in its Resolution 53 (1997), to give its opinion, to consider supporting the preparation of the final draft and to forward recommendations to the Committee of Ministers at its 5th session.

It is important to keep in mind that the Committee of Ministers is the most powerful organ in the Council of Europe. What is now the Parliamentary Assembly of the Council of Europe, formerly called the Consultative Assembly, has predominantly a consultative function. Thus, the final decisions have to be taken by the Committee of Ministers.

When I first read the preliminary Draft European Landscape Convention contained in Resolution 53 (1997), I must confess that I was very critical. The text was, I felt, rather weak: there was a lot of "considering"; I could not find the word "shall" expected in a convention. I remember that Michel Prieur was not happy with this point of view and pointed out that there was not enough political will to propose a stronger text. Like me, he would have, indeed, preferred a stronger text, but was realistic about the possibility of obtaining changes.

However, looking at the text that we are discussing today, the one adopted in Strasbourg, on 27 May 1998, I am pleased to note that it has changed for the better: we find, in many places, mandatory language, and there is an added article on implementation. I am much happier with the new draft. I also think that the removal of the proposed *ad hoc* Committee is a positive development. The new draft provides that the Committee of Ministers of the Council of Europe shall be responsible for promoting and monitoring the application of the Convention, providing political guidelines and encouragement.[8]

---

[8]   Article 10: Implementation of the Convention. Recommendation 40 (1998) on the Draft European Landscape Convention, adopted by the Congress of Local and Regional Authorities of Europe, Strasbourg, 27 May 1998.

This last draft, presented by François Paour, of France, thus represents a big change from the previous one. I agree with what Victor Ruffy said in his report to the Standing Committee: "I also think that the multidisciplinary nature of this process will enable account to be taken of the cultural and natural aspect of our landscapes in Europe and encourage commitment by territorial authorities, international governmental and non-governmental organisations and by the relevant experts".

The report proposes a draft Recommendation to the Council of Ministers, asking them to:

• consider the draft with a view to its adoption in the near future;

• associate the Parliamentary Assembly with the work of finalising this instrument;

• invite the member States to sign and ratify the Convention once it is adopted by the Committee of Ministers and;

• invite the European Union to become a party to this Convention.

Last September, the Council of Ministers mandated the Intergovernmental Committee on Nature and Environment and the Cultural Committee of the Parliamentary Assembly to consider the draft, and we can, therefore, hope for progress in the near future. Our discussions during this colloquium could still provide proposals for further improvement: at least this is what I hope.

The Draft European Landscape Convention

Jérôme Fromageau, *Président, Section Île de France, Société Française pour le Droit de l'Environnement; Vice doyen Faculté Jean Monnet, Université de Paris Sud; membre de la Commission du droit de l'environnement de l'UICN*

Monsieur le Président, vous avez déjà largement entamé la présentation des conditions dans lesquelles le projet de convention a été élaboré. Vous avez souligné les difficultés sémantiques, techniques et juridiques auxquelles le groupe d'experts a dû faire face et je ne peux que regretter l'absence de Monsieur Michael Dower, qui a fait partie de ce groupe d'experts, aidé par Monsieur Riccardo Priore, du Conseil de l'Europe, qui a montré beaucoup de ténacité pour assurer l'élaboration du projet.

Pourquoi une Convention européenne du paysage? Il y a des constats qui doivent être faits à partir de l'évaluation de Dobris sur l'environnement européen,[9] élaborée à l'occasion de la première Conférence pan-européenne des Ministres de l'environnement, qui s'est tenue à Sofia en 1995, et, celle qui a été organisée sur le thème "Un environnement pour l'Europe" à Aarhus en Juin 1998.[10] La lecture de ces évaluations est tout à fait intéressante sur le plan de l'évolution des paysages qui se réalise d'une manière particulièrement inquiétante. C'est une bonne chose que le paysage évolue mais il est moins certain que la vitesse à laquelle il se déstructure soit positive, tout particulièrement en ce qui concerne les pertes de zones humides (qui sont spectaculaires, surtout en Europe méridionale), l'augmentation de la zone forestière que se réalise au détriment de la biodiversité, l'intensification de l'agriculture, la perte en sol en raison de la bétonisation, et le développement anarchique des zones périurbaines. Ce triste bilan, qui est ainsi dressé par les experts, justifie amplement le projet de convention.

---

[9] Agence européenne de l'environnement, Sofia 1995.

[10] Quatrième Conférence ministérielle, Aarhus, Denmark, 23-25 June 1998.

Le paysage, je l'ai dit tout à l'heure, est une composante essentielle du patrimoine naturel et culturel européen dans sa grande diversité. Or, il n'y a pas d'instrument juridique international qui soit consacré directement et globalement à la gestion et à l'aménagement du paysage. Bien sûr, on peut faire un inventaire de l'ensemble des conventions qui abordent la question du paysage de manière plus on moins explicite mais toujours de façon partielle. Le projet de Convention comble donc cette lacune à l'initiative du Congrès des pouvoirs locaux et régionaux de l'Europe.

Plusieurs raisons expliquent une telle démarche:

- Il s'agit de répondre à une demande sociale et institutionnelle croissante: la protection et la gestion du paysage à l'échelle européenne nécessitant, désormais, une référence juridique internationale.

- La protection et la gestion du paysage européen représentent un intérêt qui contribue à la formation et à la consolidation de l'identité culturelle européenne. Le paysage représente, en effet, une thématique complexe qui englobe des aspects culturels et naturels et qui, dans un esprit de participation démocratique, doit tenir compte des intérêts et des exigences d'un grand nombre d'acteurs. Il est essentiel, dans toute activité concernant le paysage, d'assurer des méthodes de travail fondées sur l'interdisciplinarité, la coordination et la participation.

- Compte-tenu des exigences de démocratie ainsi que de la polyvalence et de la variété des intérêts et des valeurs paysagers à prendre en compte, il est important qu'une Convention sur le paysage puisse être conçue et élaborée au sein d'une institution représentative des intérêts des collectivités territoriales telle que le Congrès des Pouvoirs Locaux et Régionaux de l'Europe.

- La gestion des problèmes du paysage européen implique l'existence d'un instrument juridique concernant la globalité des paysages européens: instrument qui devra naturellement tenir compte des autres travaux réalisé par le Conseil de l'Europe et d'autres institutions internationales

Comme l'ont précisé C. Storelli et F. Zoido-Naranjo dans le Rapport explicatif préliminaire en vue de l'élaboration finale de la Convention, trois motifs essentiels justifient l'opportunité d'une réglementation juridique européenne du paysage:[11]

- le paysage exprime des intérêts généraux et des intérêts individuels: il existe des "intéressés" justement parce qu'il existe, et devra toujours exister, une relation paysagère entre l'être humain et le territoire qui l'entoure. Il faut établir des règles valables pour tout le monde et capables de traiter cette matière si complexe d'une façon harmonieuse et coordonnée;

- l'intérêt suscité par le paysage dépasse bien entendu toute frontière de type politico-institutionnel et pour cela il est nécessaire d'utiliser le droit européen dans sa dimension supra-nationale, valable pour tous les pays intéressés. Dans une Convention européenne du paysage doivent être reprises, en tant qu'exemples d'action, toutes les méthodes de conservation et gestion du paysage existantes dans les différents pays européens – méthodes qui dérivent d'une longue et lente prise de conscience du rôle individuel et collectif vis-à-vis de l'environnement naturel ou bâti;

- la formule de la Convention retenue est un bon instrument juridique international qui peut contraindre les pays européens à respecter et donner suite aux points fondamentaux relatifs

---

[11] *Cf* Document du Conseil de l'Europe, Congrès des pouvoirs locaux et régionaux de l'Europe, Strasbourg 12 octobre 1995, CC / CT / Pays (2) 6.

à la conservation et la gestion du paysage. La Convention sera rédigée en tenant compte de toutes les législations existantes dans les différents pays et du choix des instruments de conservation et de gestion. Chaque pays devrait pouvoir trouver dans la Convention, grâce à sa flexibilité, la manière la plus appropriée pour créer ou adapter sa propre législation. Sur la base de cette démarche, il sera peut-être alors possible d'envisager un "droit au paysage" en tant qu'expression fondamentale d'une identité culturelle européenne.

Laissant à Adrian Phillips le soin d'évoquer les aspects pratiques de la mise en oeuvre de cette future convention, je distinguerai, pour ma part, les objectifs et les mesures d'intervention.

Les objectifs

Ces objectifs visent donc, naturellement, le paysage, dont il convient de donner une définition. La détermination de celle-ci n'a pas été évidente. Effectivement, chacun des membres du groupe d'experts avait la sienne propre. Nous avons d'ailleurs tous notre définition du paysage, le juriste, le paysagiste, le géographe, l'architecte, tout comme l'élu on tout simplement le citoyen. Finalement l'article 1(a) du projet de convention précise que le *"Paysage"* est une portion de territoire, pouvant inclure les eaux côtières et/ou intérieures, telle qu'elle est perçue par les populations et dont l'aspect résulte de l'action des facteurs naturels et humains et de leurs interrelations".

Le concept d'eaux côtières et/ou intérieures a été rajouté à la demande, je crois, de l'Union mondiale pour la nature et du délégué de Malte, évidemment directement concerné. L'article 1 du Projet de convention donne une palette d'autres termes techniques qui sont définis: "protection paysagère", "gestion paysagère", "aménagement paysager", et "objectif de qualité paysagère". Le texte envisage, certes, les paysages dits remarquables, par rapport à des critères uniquement d'esthétique, mais il concerne aussi toutes les autres formes du paysage, surtout dans leur dynamique, et cela dans une perspective de développement durable. Il s'agit "d'assurer l'entretien régulier du paysage et d'harmoniser ses évolutions induites par les nécessités économiques et sociales".

Le champ d'application de la convention, il faut le souligner, concerne tout le territoire européen des parties C'est à dire une couverture géographique globale comprenant les paysages ruraux et urbains qui sont entremêlés de façon complexe. Cette convention s'applique à l'ensemble du continent européen et pourquoi pas, par extension, jusqu'à Vladivostok, comme l'a évoqué le représentant de la Russie, à la Conférence de Florence en 1998.

Les paysages peuvent être délimités par des frontières géographiques, c'est très fréquemment le cas, délimités aussi par des frontières géologiques, historiques. Cependant, la frontière n'est pas toujours un critère déterminant pour limiter un paysage. Il est donc extrêmement intéressant d'envisager des coopérations transfrontalières, cela se fait déjà relativement bien, je le rappelle, pour ce qui concerne les aires protégées.

Sur la base de cette définition du paysage et de son champ d'application, les objectifs de la convention sont pour l'essentiel au nombre de deux : d'une part, assurer la protection, la gestion et l'aménagement des paysages en Europe, par l'adoption de principes généraux et, d'autre part, consacrer juridiquement le paysage en tant que bien commun, fondement de l'identité culturelle, composante essentielle du cadre de vie, expression de la richesse et de la diversité du patrimoine.

Cette couverture géographique complète s'explique par le fait que les paysages urbains et ruraux sont entremêlés de façon complexe, que la plupart des Européens vivent dans de grandes ou de petites villes dans lesquelles la qualité des paysages exerce une forte influence sur la vie des habitants, et que les paysages ruraux revêtent un importance considérable dans la conscience européenne.

La Convention ne concernera pas seulement le domaine de la protection des sites et des paysages remarquables ou exceptionnels, mais également celui de l'aménagement de tous les paysages, car ceux-ci forment l'environnement quotidien des populations européennes. Elle exigera une attitude prospective de la part de tous ceux dont les décisions ont une incidence sur la protection, la gestion, l'amélioration ou la création de paysages. Elle aura donc des conséquences dans de très nombreux domaines relevant de la politique publique ou d'actions publiques ou privées, depuis le niveau local jusqu'au niveau européen.

Les mesures d'intervention

S'agissant des mesures d'intervention, il convient de distinguer les mesures nationales de la coopération internationale.

• ***Les mesures nationales***

Il s'agit d'abord de la connaissance du patrimoine culturel et du patrimoine naturel. On ne peut mener à bien des politiques du paysage que si l'on pose comme préalable une connaissance très poussée du problème paysager dans son ensemble, pour mieux documenter la mise en oeuvre de la planification. Parce qu'au fond, s'agissant du paysage, les plans types POS sont assez difficiles à interpréter. Le POS est une vue aérienne, mais il y a trente-six manières d'appréhender le paysage que le POS ne permet pas de saisir efficacement. Le projet de convention prend en compte, à juste titre, cette question d'inventaire d'identification des paysages, d'évaluation de la valeur de ces paysages.

Au delà de la question des inventaires, de la recherche scientifique *stricto sensu*, le projet de convention met l'accent sur l'importance de la formation et de l'éducation. Pas de politique paysagère sans la formation des techniciens et des architectes paysagistes qui font défaut dans la plupart de nos pays; sans la formation des élus aussi, cela me paraît essentiel, il suffit de voir la manière dont certains d'entre eux ont réalisé des ensembles urbains, des entrées de ville… L'éducation doit se faire dès l'école. Tout cela est explicitement visé par le projet ainsi que la participation du public. Il est en effet indispensable que les citoyens participent à l'élaboration des décisions concernant le paysage.

Des expériences significatives ont permis aux citoyens de prendre conscience de la qualité paysagère. C'est ce qui se passe par exemple pour l'élaboration des zones de protection du patrimoine architectural et paysager au sens de la législation française: les élèves des écoles, les citoyens, sont consultés pour discuter du devenir du paysage.

Au delà de cet aspect, il y a aussi, évidemment, toutes les questions qui tournent autour des techniques administratives, juridiques, fiscales et financières. La convention fournit une palette de techniques à la disposition des décideurs, des élus, pour permettre précisément une meilleure gestion du paysage.

• ***La coopération internationale***

Comme l'a rappelé le président, c'est à ce niveau que les difficultés ont été les plus difficiles à surmonter. Sans doute parce que certains Etats, et non des moindres en terme d'espace, ont pensé que cette coopération internationale risquait d'aller trop loin et de prendre une tournure un peu bureaucratique, notamment avec l'hypothétique création d'un comité européen du paysage.

La coopération internationale, c'est d'abord des échanges entre des techniciens, des programmes de formation, autant de chose que l'on sait organiser maintenant (à condition de s'en donner les moyens) et puis, c'est aussi une politique qui vise à encourager les initiatives dans le domaine de la gestion, de l'aménagement, de la protection, et pourquoi pas dans celui de la création du paysage.

Qu'est-ce que le projet de convention envisage à cet égard? D'abord un prix européen du paysage. Il a été question, à l'origine, d'un label paysager européen qui devait être accordé pour trois ans. Ce délai a été contesté et finalement les experts ont proposé un prix européen du paysage, attribué aux collectivités locales et régionales qui, dans le cadre de la politique paysagère, mettent en place des procédures de protection et de gestion tout à fait remarquables. Cette disposition est intéressante en ce qu'elle rappelle, une pratique dans le cadre de l'application d'une autre convention européenne: le Diplôme européen.

La convention prévoit aussi la création d'une "Liste des paysages d'intérêt européen présentant un intérêt significatif pour l'ensemble des populations européennes" et qui servent de modèle pour une bonne gestion. Le parallélisme entre cette nouvelle institution et les listes établies, sur les conseils de l'ICOMOS ou de l'UICN au titre de la Convention de 1972 sur le patrimoine mondial[12] est évident.

Enfin, dans la première version du projet, un Comité européen devait se charger de la mise en œuvre du suivi de l'application de la convention; finalement c'est le Comité des Ministres du Conseil de l'Europe qui va s'en charger.

Le Comité européen devait faire office de conférence des parties et, dans l'objectif des rédacteurs, cela était essentiel pour assurer l'effectivité de la convention. On ne peut que regretter l'abandon de création de cet organe. Le Comité des Ministres aura donc pour fonction de faire des recommandations sur les mesures à prendre, d'adopter des lignes directrices, de promouvoir des programmes de sensibilisation, d'encourager les programmes de protection, de gestion et d'aménagement des paysages transfrontaliers, d'arrêter la liste des paysages d'intérêt européen et enfin d'octroyer le prix européen du paysage.

Dans l'ensemble, l'adoption d'une telle convention régionale sur le paysage me paraît s'imposer dans le sens souhaité par le Congrès des pouvoirs locaux et régionaux de l'Europe, instance du Conseil de l'Europe, représentative des collectivités territoriales. Ceci est significatif de la prise de conscience des collectivités territoriales en faveur de la qualité paysagère, facteur d'identité et de développement économique et de qualité de la vie en général.

Cette convention constituera, de par son caractère flexible, que certains lui reprocheront peut-être, une référence juridique générale, pour l'ensemble des pays européens. La variété des intérêts à prendre en compte et la diversité des actions à mettre en œuvre, selon le type de paysage considéré justifient, à n'en pas douter, un telle souplesse. Elle contribuera à la formation et à la consolidation de l'identité culturelle européenne.

Commentator: *Donna Craig, Vice Chair, IUCN Commission on Environmental Law; Professor, Faculty of Law, Macquarie University, Australia*

Mr. Fromageau has given considerable insight into what appears as modern environmental law for someone from the other end of the world: my home is Australia. The approach of the European Landscape Convention is important because it integrates natural, cultural, social and economic values and puts an emphasis on the aesthetic values. It conveys the idea that, in a sense, sustainable development and environmental protection do not have boundaries and it incorporates sustainable use elements. This integration is crucial to modern international and domestic environmental law.

---

[12] *Cf supra at N. 3.*

I have the privilege of coming from an island, an island nation. In Australia, we have to deal with transboundary problems because Australia's federal system has nine state and territory jurisdictions. Many of the disputes that you have across nations we have across state borders within our country. Thus, the need for discussion about values, cooperation and management is very much at the heart of federal systems as well.

I have spent much of my professional and personal life trying to support the aspirations and values of indigenous, tribal and local communities. One thing I have learned from this experience is that indigenous peoples and local communities do not like terminology such as boundaries and territories because their conception of cultural boundaries, their conception of management and value cannot be put within border constraints. For example, in Australia, under aboriginal law, the areas and places for which aboriginal people are responsible do not coincide with their tribal responsibility. The obligation to take care of the country is personal to the aboriginal custodian and, in fact, no one else can speak for the country, except the custodian. The tribe or the Tribal Council, in the terminology of other places, has no right under aboriginal law to speak for that country.

Setting up parks and management processes that are not in accordance with these responsibilities and do not reflect these values has often very tragic consequences. I am, therefore, very interested in the attempts to integrate the cultural and natural dimensions and in the way in which the Draft European Landscape Convention tries to deal with these issues. The model provided by this particular draft convention can be used to approach the same type of issues under other jurisdictions.

To demonstrate how this may occur I shall use an example from my country. We have a very valuable World Heritage Site, the Kakadu National Park, with one uranium mine already, where there have been 93 incidents of breaches of environmental standards. There is a proposal for another uranium mine in the region, against the wishes of the aboriginal custodians. Constantly, throughout this dispute, the aboriginal owners have said that their cultural boundaries in no way coincide with the World Heritage site boundaries or the Australian Park boundaries. It is important to find ways of giving recognition to the aboriginal cultural values in the Australian management processes and in the constitution of national parks and world heritage sites.

I can only praise the wonderful approach of the Draft European Landscape Convention to an integrated transboundary law which is aimed at sustainable development in the modern sense.

Practical Considerations for the Implementation of a European Landscape Convention

Adrian Phillips, Chair, IUCN World Commission on Protected Areas; former Director General of the Countryside Commission of England and Wales; Professor, Cardiff University, UK

This paper will:

- consider the significance of landscape generally, and of European landscapes in particular;

- review the problems facing the landscapes of Europe; and

- summarise in layman's terms the implications of the Draft European Landscape Convention

Landscape

Landscape had not received as much attention from environmental policy makers, and environmental lawyers, as has nature conservation, pollution control and abatement, and land use. Certainly until recently it has not been the subject of much international debate. But that is changing. Inclusion of "cultural landscapes" within the scope of the World Heritage Convention a few years ago (Rossler, 1995), the treatment of landscapes as a separate issue in the Dobris assessment (Stanners and Bordeau, eds. 1995), the identification of the landscapes as an action theme in the Pan-European Biological and Landscape Diversity Strategy (Council of Europe, 1996), and now the possibility of a European convention on landscape are specific important developments. They suggest that landscape, as a focus for public policy, is moving on to the international agenda.

Why should that be? The key lies in interaction between people and nature which is at the core of the idea of landscape. This is apparent in the definition offered in the draft European Landscape Convention "Landscape is a piece of territory which may include coastal and/or inland waters, as perceived by populations, the appearance of which is determined by the action and inter-action of natural and human factors".

Landscape, defined in these terms, has certain distinctive characteristics.

- it contains both natural and cultural values and features, and focuses on the relationships between these;

- it is both physical and metaphysical, with social, cultural and artistic associations. While landscape is how we see the world, it is thus more than mere scenery and appearance. We take it in with all our senses;

- while we can experience landscape only in the present, it is the sum of all past changes to the environment: it is where past and present meet; and

- landscape gives identity to place, and hence diversity to the settings of our lives.

Since landscape is about seeing the world as "nature plus people", it has a particular resonance in the post-Rio period. If sustainable development has any generally agreed meanings, it is surely that we should pursue human well-being and environmental protection together, not at each others' expense; and that we need a holistic approach to the management of the development process, embracing economic, social, cultural and ecological considerations. Landscapes are a framework within which this can be done.

Indeed it can be argued that "landscape" is much more likely to concern the man in the street, or the woman in the field, than is "biodiversity". Landscapes, whether distinguished or degraded – provide the settings for our lives. Landscape explicitly recognises that people have a place in the environment, interacting with nature. It is thus a means of linking people to nature, treating them as part of the natural world and not apart from it. It appeals to our sense of history and continuity. "Reading" landscapes is a way of understanding how our ancestors survived and shaped the world around them. Thus landscape provides a connection to our past. And it is a way in which people can find identity and distinctiveness; thus it provides a sense of place.

Indeed, landscape has numerous values and functions for society. For example, many landscapes are important because they demonstrate the sustainable use of natural resources (e.g. the agro-silvo-pastural landscapes of the Montado and Dehesa in the Iberian peninsula, the sheep grass downlands of Southern Britain, or the Puszta of Hungary) and thus help us to understand how to manage such places in future. Such extensively farmed or grazed landscapes are very important for their biodiversity, particularly so in the absence of true wilderness areas in most parts of Europe: indeed the Natura 2000 network will contain many such places, and nature will only survive in them if they are managed as working landscapes.

Landscapes also have important economic values, particularly those which, because of their quality and variety, are the foundations for successful tourism and recreation industries upon which many jobs and local incomes depend; or, looked at from the users' point of view, such landscapes provide cultural, recreational and aesthetic experiences for people who have to spend most of their lives within the much more controlled environments of our cities. Indeed the role of landscapes as a setting for enhancing the physical health and mental well-being of urban populations is hugely important. Landscapes are also significant for the cultural elements which they contain, such as ancient field systems or vernacular farm buildings. And of course they often have great cultural significance of another kind through their associations with literature, painting and music.

The richness and diversity of landscapes in Europe is a particular feature of this region of the world. "There is probably nowhere else where the signs of human interaction with nature in landscape are so varied, contrasting and localised" (Stanners and Bordeau, 1995, p. 172). Despite that, hitherto landscapes have been regarded very much as a national or even a local responsibility, and their emergence on the European scale has only been recent. There is now growing recognition that:

• all countries face pressures on their landscapes, and need to share experience in dealing with these;

• in Europe at any rate, it is artificial to try to pursue European biodiversity conservation objectives (e.g. through Natura 2000), without a parallel involvement in landscape management;

• many of the pressures upon the landscape arise at a European scale and need to be tackled at that level (e.g. the CAP); and

• as Europeans travel more, they have perhaps an increasing sense of shared ownership of those places which they recognise as truly outstanding landscapes.

The Problems Facing European Landscapes

Since landscape is the result of interaction between people and nature, it follows that when the character of that interaction changes, the landscape is inevitably altered. Europe is intensely populated, settled and used by humankind: the demands which its people place upon the land for food, timber, minerals, water supplies, building land, tourism and recreation, transport systems and so forth have all to be met within the landscape and are bound to have a major impact upon the landscape.

There are some examples of such late twentieth century development demands leading to new and better landscapes, but in general most modern development has been large in scale, insensitive in design and dominating in its impact. As a result it diminishes the quality of the landscape. This is most apparent when we look at the results of intensified agriculture, very evident in Western Europe. Now, through the eastwards extension of the Common Agricultural Policy, this is threatening to have a similar impact on the remaining traditional landscapes of Central and Eastern Europe which survived the devastating impact of collective farming under communist rule. Architectural styles and local materials, which give distinctive character to local landscapes, are too often replaced by standardised designs and materials. And of course many of the coastal, lakeside and mountain areas which have a particular landscape appeal have suffered from unsympathetic tourism development.

In contrast to the pressures of development, other landscapes have suffered through abandon-ment and neglect. In some remoter mountainous regions around the Mediterranean basin and other areas, carefully tended farming systems, e.g. terracing, have broken down and the land reverted to scrub, buildings have become derelict and the whole landscape is deteriorating. Landscapes around cities are also vulnerable to abandonment, as traditional land uses become impossible to maintain under pressures from nearby urban centres.

A third group of problems are those associated with pollution and misuse of the resources of land, air and water. Sometimes these are fairly localised, but long range pollution (such as that caused by acid rain) has an impact on forest landscapes throughout Europe. Excessive abstraction lowers water tables with damaging impact on wetland vegetation; so too does the canalisation of rivers. Insidious forms of pollution affect soil, freshwater and coastal areas – and all have an impact on the landscape. Climate change and rising sea levels are also bound to have a far reaching landscape effect.

In summary the pressures described above are inducing changes, some subtle and some obvious; some occurring gradually, some with great speed – the combined effect of which is:

- the degradation of distinctive landscape features;

- the diminution of natural and cultural values; and

- the weakening, and even breaking, of the links between people and the land.

"The overall result is that the diversity, distinctiveness and value of many landscapes in Europe are declining rapidly" (Stanners and Bordeau, p. 186)

The policy challenge which we face therefore is how to ensure the survival of Europe's rich heritage of landscapes in a period of accelerating economic and social change. At the heart of this challenge is a dilemma. Landscape reflects the way that human needs are pursued in the environmental context; apart from a very few "museum landscapes", it is therefore unrealistic to try to "freeze" a landscape at some particular time in its long evolution. The goal rather should be to manage the process of change. This means aiming to reduce the damaging effect of activities on the landscape, and on the natural and cultural values which it contains, and at the same time encouraging the creation of new landscape values. The objective should be to sustain and even enrich the diversity and quality of Europe's landscapes within the context of social and economic development. This is the challenge which the Draft Landscape Convention seeks to address.

The Draft European Landscape Convention

The draft convention is based on three principles:

- recognition of the value and importance of the landscapes to the people of Europe;

- belief that it is possible to guide the process of change affecting landscapes so that variety, diversity and quality are enhanced; and

- conviction that people must be involved in making this happen.

The Draft Convention seeks to build on these principles by promoting actions at the national and at the European level.

At the national level, the first need is to raise public and professional awareness of landscape. Landscape is a peoples' issue. Everyone's quality of life is affected by the landscapes around, and everyone – farmer, forester, house-owner or industrialist – can by their own actions make an impact on the landscape in their care. This is why the Draft Convention seeks to establish the legal principle that the landscape is an essential component of the surroundings of human populations, an expression of their shared heritage and the foundation of their identity. At a more practical level, it commits parties to undertake information and awareness campaigns for the public. Four audiences are particularly important: young people, farmers and landowners, professionals and decision makers. Landscapes should be included as a cross-cutting theme in school education: it is relevant to the teaching of history, geography, natural sciences and the arts, and it is the ideal outdoor classroom. Farmers and landowners are the principal architects of the landscape: they need advice and support if they are to be encouraged to maintain and invest in the landscapes of the future. Professionals in fields as varied as planning, civil engineering, land management and agriculture all need to absorb the significance of landscape in their work. Decision makers and elected officials who authorise, or reject, the policies, programmes and projects which help to shape the landscape of the future, also need to be aware of their responsibilities.

Public awareness should be built upon knowledge about our landscapes. In some countries such as Sweden (Sporron, 1995), Ireland (Aalen, 1997) and England (Countryside Commission 1997), nation-wide work has been undertaken to survey, record and understand landscapes. Some pioneer work of this kind has also been done at the European level (e.g. Stanners and Bordeau, 1995, Chapter 8). What such exercises have in common is a focus on identifying the distinctive character of each area, with its natural and manmade elements (the technique is sometimes called Landscape Character Analysis). The power of such analytical work has been greatly enhanced in recent years by technical advances in survey, including remote sensing and GIS mapping; and also by the results of cross-disciplinary research in institutions across Europe which have drawn out the connections between ecological and historical aspects of the landscape. Such landscape character information is a prerequisite for the evaluation of landscapes, that is the process of informed judgement about what is distinctive in each landscape, and where landscape improvement should be sought. In the spirit of the Draft Convention, this should be done by professionals working with the local communities who live in the landscape concerned.

The final strand of national action is the most far reaching: definition of policies and their implementation for each landscape area. The Convention draws a most useful distinction between policies for three purposes: protection, management and planning.

Landscape protection is defined as "action to preserve a landscape's existing features, justified by its outstanding value". Landscape protection is an appropriate policy for a country's finest landscapes, and many countries have indeed designed protected areas for this purpose. IUCN recognises these as protected landscapes/seascapes or Category V in its system of Protected Area Management Categories (IUCN, 1994).

Landscape management is defined as "action to ensure the regular upkeep of a landscape and to harmonise changes necessary for economic and social reasons". Michael Dower calls this "a process of deliberate stewardship to maintain the quality and diversity of each landscape and prevent its erosion by abandonment, neglect and abuse". Landscape management is a suitable approach for most areas, certainly for the great tracts of rural Europe where the landscapes, though not outstanding, still retain their distinctive qualities.

Landscape planning has the aim of "creating new landscapes" through a process of plan-making, design and construction. Landscape planning is about landscape enhancement and is suitable for areas which have been left derelict from past industrialisation, degraded by intensive agriculture or subjected to a whole range of pressures in peri-urban areas. Landscape planning is a conscious investment in landscape enhancement for future generations, for example through the creation of new forests around cities.

Of course, in any single area it is likely that a mix of these approaches will be appropriate but in general the scale "landscape protection-landscape management-landscape planning" is appropriate to "outstanding-moderate-degraded landscapes". Thereby the point is made that all landscapes are appropriate for landscape policies, from the finest scenery of remote mountains and coastal areas to the degraded environment around our cities.

National and local implementation of landscape policies can be achieved through a range of familiar instruments:

- Land use planning

- Regulation

- Public works

- Incentives

- Ownership

- Partnership

- Special status for special areas

Systems of land use planning are common throughout Europe, combining two approaches: plans, which are medium and long term frameworks for directing, stimulating or discouraging development, changes in land use, provision for infrastructure etc.; and controls over land use, construction etc. Thus plan making provides the strategic framework for landscape policy. Land use plans should be based on a sound knowledge of landscape values, used for landscape protection, management and planning, and developed through a process of securing public support. Development control, an exercise which touches people in every country, is the regulatory tactic by which landscape policies are achieved, ranging from modest requirements upon house builders to respect vernacular styles and use local materials, to the incorporation of landscape considerations in environmental impact assessments which help determine the acceptability of major infrastructure, tourism or mineral projects for example.

The EC and national, regional and local governments fund public programs of many kinds across the face of Europe. Landscape considerations should be taken into account in the shaping of these, for example, in state forestry programmes, where mono-culture regimes are giving way to a more sensitive mixture of species and programmes for planting and felling. Landscape factors should be used to help shape the location or routing of major infrastructure projects such as roads, railways and reservoirs, and then to determine the detailed way in which they are planned into the landscape. The same considerations should apply to projects for energy generation and transmission, and mineral extraction.

Many of the most highly valued landscapes of Europe were created through traditional patterns of land use and reflect traditional ways of life in the European countryside. Their survival depends upon the continuation, in modern form, of the ways of life which created them. This cannot be done by regulation, nor can it be done by leaving rural communities in a state of poverty (this is morally unacceptable, of course, but in any case people will migrate from the land). The preferred approach is to recognise and support these aspects of traditional land use, which produce landscapes of high environmental value. It also requires the underpinning of the local economy whilst making it capable of adapting to changed markets, and particularly exploiting the economic values inherent in traditional landscapes (for example, through tourism or craft industries). The EC's Agri-Environmental Programme of incentives for land owners and occupiers aims to do this. In some countries, too, tax incentives are available for this purpose.

Many of Europe's most highly valued landscapes (including key mountain, coast and lakeside areas) are in public, quasi-public or voluntary body ownership, as a mark of their importance to the public. The owners have a particular opportunity and responsibility to manage such land in an exemplary way, thus demonstrating high standards of environment and landscape care, and to make such areas available for appropriate public access.

Even when outright ownership is not practical, public bodies can enter into partnerships with owners and occupiers of land to implement programmes of landscape care and enhancement. Though ultimate recourse to regulation may still be necessary, successful partnerships for landscapes depend primarily on a mix of incentives and rewards on one hand and education, advice and recognition on the other. Many European countries have devised mechanisms to underpin such partnerships, such as management agreements, legally binding covenants and other forms of mutual undertakings.

Finally at the national level, special status can be accorded to certain landscapes so as to ensure that they become the focus of attention, e.g. through targeted financial and other support, by particular measures for landscape protection, management or planning, or by the setting up of a special agency to take charge of the area's management. Two kinds of landscape are particularly appropriate for such approaches: outstanding landscapes which should be given protected area status; and grossly degraded landscapes which require particular concentration and effort to achieve lasting landscape improvements.

At the international level, the Draft Convention proposes to complement the national level of landscape protection, management and planning with a European-wide set of actions. These are of four kinds:

- support for national effort;

- support for transfrontier landscapes;

- recognition of outstanding achievements in landscape protection, management and planning;

- recognition of landscapes of European significance.

As recognised above, most landscape work must, of course, be undertaken at the national or local level, but the Convention acknowledges that European landscapes are a common resource, for whose protection, management and planning they have a duty to cooperate. Co-operation should: cover all technical and scientific aspects of landscape protection, management and planning; involve exchange amongst the staff engaged in landscape work around Europe; include exchange of experience on the implementation of the Convention itself; and promote public awareness and understanding of landscape issues at the European scale.

One particular area of interest is collaboration in the protection and management of transfrontier landscapes. Many European countries share common areas of landscape with their neighbours (mountain ranges or river valleys in particular). It is desirable that work on one side of the boundary should be coordinated with that on the other. In some cases this can be done through the framework of agreements already established between neighbouring protected areas. But the scope for collaboration extends far beyond that, and the Convention could be an effective way of encouraging such transfrontier cooperation.

One important role of the Draft Convention is to promote higher standards in landscape protection, management and planning. The proposed European Landscape Prize would be a way of conferring such distinction, recognising outstandingly successful efforts and promoting them as examples to be followed elsewhere in Europe. Its award would carry with it a commitment to continued high standards in the care of the area.

The landscape prize is to be given for the quality of landscape management. But the Convention also introduces the idea of a list of Landscapes of European Significance as an award for the quality of the landscape itself. Based upon criteria to be drawn up and agreed by the Committee of Ministers, the countries of Europe would be invited to nominate areas which are regarded as outstanding in terms of landscape quality. Examples might include the Puzsta of the Hungarian plains, the hills of Umbria and Tuscany in the Northern Apennines, the valleys of the Lot, Tarn and Dordogne of South West France, the waterways vistas of the Netherlands or Lake District in Northern England. Such areas have inspired writers and artists, drawn travellers and achieved fame far beyond the immediate locality. As Michael Dower says "if the conservation of Venice, Granada or Prague is in a sense a European concern, so too should be that of such important landscapes". As with the Landscape Prize, transfrontier landscapes could be included, provided all concerned countries submit a joint request. But it is essential that any landscapes that are nominated have already been recognised as significant at the national level, and that the countries concerned commit themselves to continued protection. Arrangements would be put in place for the removal of landscapes from the list should it be determined that they no longer meet the criteria for inclusion.

This concept of landscapes of European significance would of course complement the World Heritage Status which UNESCO has recently extended to the field of cultural landscapes. Thus it would put in place a three tier level of recognition, landscapes of national importance (normally identified as protected landscapes, i.e. Category V), landscapes of European significance (recognised under the proposed Landscape Convention), and cultural landscapes of "outstanding universal value" recognised under the World Heritage Convention. The Draft Convention has been welcomed by the World Heritage Centre as complementing the World Heritage Convention's efforts at the global scale by putting in place also a regional level of landscape recognition.

Despite the importance of the idea of landscapes of European significance, it is worth repeating that in general the Draft Convention is about all landscapes; it is deliberately comprehensive and relevant to the setting of everyone's life. Its philosophy can be captured in the phrase "nowhere is nowhere, and everywhere is somewhere".

Conclusion

As we have seen, landscape has only recently emerged as a suitable area for international attention, and there is much to be learnt about landscapes and their protection, management and planning. The proponents of the draft convention are realistic about what it can achieve. Certainly it cannot

---

References

Aalen F. (ed.) (1997) *Atlas of the Irish Rural Landscape* Cork University Press

Council for Europe (1996) *The Pan European Biological and Landscape Strategy* COE, Strasbourg

Countryside Commission (1997) *The Character of England: landscape, wildlife and natural features* Cheltenham, UK

IUCN and WCMC (1994) *Guidelines on Protected Area Management Categories* IUCN, Cambridge

McCloskey C. (1996) *PEBLDS Explained* IIED, London

Rossler M. (1995) UNESCO and Cultural Landscape Protection in Von Droste B, Plachter H. and Rossler M (eds.) *Cultural Landscapes of Universal Value* Gustav Fischer, Jena

Sporron (ed.) (1995) *Swedish Landscapes Swedish Environmental Protection Agency*, Stockholm

Stanners D. and Bourdeau P. (eds.) (1995) *Europe's Environment: the Dobris Assessment* European Environment Agency, Copenhagen

hope to turn round all the trends leading to the continent-wide erosion of landscape values and the loss of landscape variety and diversity. Nor is it the only means of addressing this problem at the European scale: there is also Action Theme 4 of the Pan-European Biological and Landscape Diversity Strategy (PBLDS), to which the Draft Convention can make a very specific contribution, the European Spatial Development Perspective and the reform of the CAP, to mention three important initiatives affecting landscape. But the unique role of the Convention, if it is implemented with the same kind of vigour and enthusiasm that has marked its development, would be that it could set the countries of Europe down the road to understand better, and value more highly, their individual and shared landscape heritage; and help them to put in place policies, which enjoy public support, for the improved care of the landscape.

Commentator: *Cyrille de Klemm, membre de la Commission du droit de l'environnement de l'UICN; Vice Président, Société française pour le droit de l'environnement*

Quelque réflexions très rapides sur la manière de faire fonctionner la Convention lorsqu'elle sera en vigueur, ce que nous espérons tous, mais qui pour le moment n'est encore malheureusement pas certain.

Je crois que le coeur de la Convention est son article 9. Je vous rappelle que cet article nous dit que : "chaque partie s'engage à mettre en place les moyens d'intervention, visant la protection, la gestion et/ou l'aménagement des paysages qui auront été identifiés et évalués." Et ensuite la convention renvoie à son annexe, qui contient une liste, d'ailleurs non exhaustive, des différents types d'instruments juridiques ou financiers qui pourraient être ainsi utilisés pour protéger les paysages. Comme l'a rappelé Adrian Phillips, il y a trois aspects majeurs : la protection, la gestion, et l'aménagement de la nature. Cette liste d'instruments, qu'Adrian Phillips a qualifié d'instruments familiers, je ne suis pas si certain qu'ils soient familiers, surtout en ce qui concerne le paysage; ce sont des instruments qui sont utilisés en droit de l'urbanisme, ou en droit de protection de la nature, pour protéger des espaces ou des espèces, ou bien des habitats d'espèces, mais ils sont encore rarement utilisés pour protéger le paysage.

Je peux vous donner des exemples: il n'est pas facile de trouver des instruments qui fonctionnent pour contrôler, par exemples, des boisements intempestifs (afforestation) ou bien la destruction de la végétation naturelle. Je crois que nous devrions nous engager dans une réflexion un petit peu en profondeur sur les types d'instruments qui sont mentionnés dans l'annexe de la Convention et puis, comme ce n'est pas une liste exhaustive, sur tout autre type d'instruments qui pourrait exister et qui serait utilisable, ou tout autre type d'instruments que nous pourrions peut-être inventer, pourquoi pas ? Et voir dans quelle mesure les instruments existants doivent être adaptés pour protéger le paysage en général et peut-être, plus particulièrement, certains éléments du paysage. Ceci est donc un premier aspect.

Le deuxième aspect, c'est l'aspect institutionnel. Là-dessus la Convention est totalement muette. Elle ne nous parle absolument pas d'institutions, de ce qui doit être organisé dans les différents pays pour la faire fonctionner. En cela elle a probablement raison, c'est une affaire qui concerne les parties, et elle doit être réglée au niveau national. Mais nous, nous n'avons pas besoin de nous limiter à cela, il serait peut-être utile que nous examinions quels sont les types d'institutions qui sont les plus à même de permettre la mise en application effective de la Convention. Il ne faut pas nous limiter aux institutions nationales parce que, l'essentiel de ce qui va se passer pour protéger les paysages, va se passer au niveau local. Il faut là aussi des structures et des gens qui s'en occupent, parce qu'autrement il ne se passera évidemment pas grand chose.

Ainsi, on pourrait se demander si un plan d'occupation des sols, municipal ou local, ne pourrait pas en même temps être un plan de conservation du paysage. Ce n'est pas le cas à l'heure actuelle, mais c'est quelque chose que l'on pourrait imaginer: comment transformer cet instrument d'urbanisme pour qu'il fonctionne, en même temps, comme instrument paysager.

Donc, peut-être pourrions-nous faire un inventaire et porter des jugements sur les instruments existants. Nous demander s'il ne serait pas possible de lancer des projets pilotes et essayer de trouver aussi de nouvelles idées pour l'avenir. De cette façon, lorsque la Convention entrera en vigueur, une partie du travail que son secrétariat aurait probablement à faire, sera déjà fait, ce qui permettra de gagner beaucoup de temps, si nous arrivions à identifier des instruments efficaces.

Dans ce sens, peut-être, permettez-moi simplement de lancer d'idée: pourrait-on imaginer un projet conjoint entre la Commission de droit de l'UICN et sa Commission des aires protégées, sans exclure d'autres commissions de l'UICN. Cela nous permettrait de gagner beaucoup de temps. Quand la Convention sera en vigueur, et déjà cela prendra un certain nombre d'années, il faudra une longue période de rodage avant qu'elle n'ait suffisamment de parties, avant que son secrétariat ne soit suffisamment efficace, avant que les travaux de recherche et les études nécessaires aient été faites. Si une partie de ce travail était faite d'avance, cela nous permettrait, probablement, de sauver un certain nombre de paysages.

Pan-European Biological and Landscape Diversity Strategy

Elisabeth Hopkins, *Acting Director, IUCN European Regional Office*

Thank you to the organisers, for inviting me here. It is a pleasure to meet people from two IUCN Commissions in one place at one time, to be in this beautiful building and to be in Paris.

Françoise Burhenne-Guilmin has mentioned the multidisciplinary nature of IUCN. And I am going to try and inject, in my presentation, a little bit of the politics that lie behind environmental decision making and environmental policy formation in a Pan-European context.

I have been invited to speak about the Pan-European Biological and Landscape Diversity Strategy (PBLDS). It is a long name, in the English speaking world, we now affectionately call it PBLDS. I am afraid there is no easy acronym in French, or, indeed, in Spanish. I hope the translators do not interpret it as *"les cailloux"*! So if you forgive me, I'll continue to call it PBLDS for the purpose of this presentation, which will look at what PBLDS does and how it might be used to promote and take forward ideas of landscape conservation in Europe.

I shall begin by placing PBLDS in its wider context, in what is known as the Environment for Europe process. I shall then try to tackle the questions of what it is, how it works, and what might be its future.

The Environment for Europe process is a truly astonishing initiative of regional and inter-regional cooperation on the environment. It was the brainchild of the former Czechoslovak Environment Minister Josef Vavrasek, who was sadly killed in an avalanche, in his beloved Tatra Mountains in 1994.

The process brings together some 54 countries, of what is called the Pan-European region, to discuss environmental policy. After several years of discussion, the regional consensus is finally reached and expressed at ministerial meetings. These have been held in 1991, 1993, 1995 and most recently in Aarhus, Denmark, this year. The next ministerial meeting will be held in Ukraine in the year 2002.

The process was conceived as an expression of the "Common European Home", which owes much to the progressive thinking and hopes of dissident groups in Central Europe. We might ask why was environment chosen for this unique process? This is partly because environment became the relatively politically safe basis on which to challenge the former regimes. And as we know, in some parts of the Central and Eastern European regions, devastated landscapes were visible for all to see.

The overall process has, in my view, certain characteristics which help to comprehend PBLDS and, more particularly, help us to understand how we could use PBLDS to further our objectives. The Pan-European process is political in inspiration: western governments quickly used it to introduce regional cooperation, pluralism, democracy, market principles and instruments to underlie environmental policy. Non-governmental organisations (NGOs), including IUCN, have always played a significant role in the process. Beneath the upper political layer, however, it is probably true that environmental strategy and policy-making have been accelerated with the transition in Central and Eastern European countries, thanks to the various activities within the process. PBLDS is one of those strands of activity.

The final point I wish to make on the broader context for PBLDS is that the Aarhus ministerial meeting, the fourth on the Environment for Europe series, perhaps marks a turning point. At Aarhus, a Convention on public participation and access to information was signed by most of the participating countries.[13] Not only is this the first regional convention on public participation in the world, it has also shown that a process which has so far been characterised as "soft" in nature, can also have a "harder" side to it and can, in fact, sponsor international law. This has obvious implications for promoting and adopting a convention on landscapes. A point worthy of note is that NGOs, including IUCN represented by Dr. Wolfgang Burhenne, played a crucial and much praised role in initiating, developing and actually negotiating the Aarhus Convention.

The points I want to make here, in relation to this meeting are the following:

- the PBLDS is part of a primarily politically inspired process;

- the process has shown, in 1998, that it can produce hard international law, in the shape of a Convention;

- the role of NGOs is recognised and substantive.

The future of this process is a little uncertain for the moment, but we should recognise that it is likely to fragment with the accession of ten more Central European countries, bringing new borders within Europe. The process is moving further East: the next meeting will be in Ukraine, a so-called newly independent State, and probably we can expect to see a future ministerial meeting in Central Asia.

Pan-European Strategy or PBLDS

The strategy was endorsed by Ministers at the Third Pan-European meeting in Sofia, Bulgaria, in 1995. The Council of Europe, with UNEP, provide the secretariat, IUCN and OECD are named in the Sofia Ministerial Declaration as privileged partners.

The main objective of the PBLDS is to provide an innovative and proactive approach to stop and reverse the degradation of biological and landscape diversity values in Europe. It is increasingly seen as a regional instrument to support implementation of the Convention on Biological Diversity. It seeks to coordinate actions and provide synergies to achieve its objectives. It is coming to the close of its first five-year action plan, which lasts to the year 2000. It comprises twelve Action Themes, Theme number 4 deals with the conservation of landscapes.

---

[13] UNECE, Convention on Access to Information, Public Participation in Decision-Making and Access to Justice in Environmental Matters, "Aarhus Convention", adopted at ECE, 4th Ministerial Conference, "Environment for Europe", Aarhus, Denmark, 25 June 1998, E-ECE-1366.

Under Action Theme 4 an action plan has been developed by the lead organisations in cooperation with others. The aim of the action plan is to develop a European and integrated approach to landscape conservation and management in order to further the conservation and adequate management of the qualities of landscapes of European importance. Actions under the plan can be summarised according to four headings:

- analytical projects including landscape typologies, landscape assessment criteria, driving forces for land use change, identifying conflict zones, etc.;

- a series of priority setting projects, geographical and thematic issues of European importance – some of the work has been applied to the very difficult discussions on changes in European agricultural policy that are taking place now;

- public awareness and education;

- integration, conservation and conflict management.

From documents I have reviewed for this presentation and conversations I have had, there appears to be little real collaboration or connection between the work being done under Action Theme 4 of the PBLDS and the Draft European Landscape Convention. Indeed the Council of Europe's own progress report states: "in addition to the activities carried out in the frame of the strategy, a draft European Landscape Convention is being prepared". This indicates that the Convention is not considered as part of the strategy. While the activities under the strategy are mainly analytical and policy-oriented, the activities for the Convention take place in another framework, that of the Council of Europe's Congress of Local and Regional Authorities. This gap should, and can, surely be overcome and bridged over the next few years.

Following the evolution of the overall Environment for Europe process, the PBLDS will probably also move toward the East; this has to be taken into account if landscapes are to be discussed further under the PBLDS. There will probably be calls from Governments and NGOs to reduce the number of Action Themes from 12 to perhaps 3 or 4. There is already a consensus building to focus on Action Theme 02 on National Strategies; Action Theme 1 on Ecological Networks; Action Theme 2 about integration of biodiversity into economic sectors and Action Theme 3 which is the cross-cutting one of Raising Awareness. I have not heard mention of Action Theme 4, on landscapes, as one of the selected *foci*, but this could change.

The future of PBLDS will be discussed at the next Council Meeting which will be held in March 1999. I would suggest that the best strategy for maintaining a landscape interest under PBLDS is to explore links with the popular Action Themes, in addition to exploring links with the Draft Convention. It seems that PBLDS has not always taken all the opportunities offered by its position in the Environment for Europe process. A group of NGOs, including IUCN, are engaged in analysing why this is the case. Our paper will be presented to the PBLDS Council next March.

I think that while the detailed work on the landscape theme and on other themes has taken into account the key political and economic concerns in the region, such as agriculture, the future World Trade Organisation negotiations, or the declining health status in Central and Eastern European countries, the Strategy has not been able to make the links and build the coalition that is needed to raise the profile of its actions on the political stage. We nearly did not have any biodiversity at the recent meeting in Aarhus, one argument being, from some Governments: "We have heard it all before", as if it was a sector that can be taken or left as we please. To me this signifies that there is a lot of work to be done in explaining the importance of biodiversity and, indeed, landscape.

In conclusion, if you see the PBLDS as a vehicle for furthering the landscape concerns of IUCN and other organisations gathered here, it will be necessary to gain political support. The way forward has already been pointed out in some of the earlier presentations. Landscapes do help to forward cooperation between countries, landscapes do help to define a European identity, and this would correspond very closely to the background political drive behind the overall Environment for Europe process. I believe that it is important for the PBLDS process to link more closely into the Convention process. I wonder whether Action Theme 4 could provide scientific and policy support to help monitor the implementation of the Convention and to improve the way in which it is conceived and received by Governments in Europe.

Commentator: *Oleg Kolbasov, Vice Chair, IUCN Commission on Environmental Law; Professor, Institute of State and Law, Russian Federation; Head, Centre for Ecological Law, Eurasia*

I have no special comments on the Pan-European Biological and Landscape Strategy itself, but wish to present a brief survey of the current situation in the countries of the Commonwealth of Independent States (CIS) region, taking into account perspectives for the implementation of the Strategy in this region.

The Pan-European Strategy is much appreciated as an instrument for protection and rational use of the natural environment in our countries, including landscape and biodiversity values. But I would like to underline that at present this Strategy is known only by a limited number of people in these countries. Only experts from the State Agencies dealing with environmental protection and some members of Non-Governmental Organisations specialising in ecology are acquainted with it. The text of the Strategy has not been published in Russian for wide distribution, the public is not involved in its implementation and it is very well known that, without public participation, it can hardly be expected that the Strategy be implemented successfully and timely. In this respect, it is important that priority be given to the task of explaining the sense of the Strategy to the public in our countries.

I would like to underline that CIS countries have a long experience in preserving biological and landscape diversity. Certainly, there may be some shortcomings, but we must make concessions for local conditions. Forms and methods for conservation have been developing for decades and are well known to the population. It is necessary to take them into account and incorporate them in the implementation of the Strategy. As the need arises, new forms and methods for preserving the biological and landscape diversity can be introduced.

At the same time, we have a rather developed environmental legislation, including a number of provisions in Constitutions and special laws which may be used for the protection of landscape and biological diversity.

The Constitutions of CIS countries contain provisions relating to environmental protection which encompass the issues of biological and landscape diversity. They particularly provide that any type of ownership cannot be used in a manner detrimental to the environment.

National legislation concerning protection and use of lands, waters, mineral resources, wildlife, forests and plant life is available. Special laws on protected areas, on recreation lands around human settlements, on medicinal resources and medicinal areas and on water protection zones are also in force. Regional and local agencies are given administrative powers for allocating and protecting natural resources. Thus, selected provisions of the Pan-European Biological and Landscape Diversity Strategy can be implemented.

We are particularly devoted to specially protected areas, and under this legislation a lot of positive steps have been taken. For example, if we turn to Action Theme 1: "Establishing Pan-European Ecological Network" it is useful to note that, in recent years, new laws on specially protected areas have been adopted in the CIS countries. They provide for conservation of pristine, vast, natural complexes. Natural reserves, national and regional parks, zakazniks and monuments of nature are established on these areas. In the Russian Federation, for example, we have some 100 natural reserves, 30 national parks, 10 regional parks, 1600 zakazniks, 7500 monuments of nature, covering in total some 3% of the territory of Russia.

Landscape protection is provided for by the legislation on town planning, land use, forests and water codes. The Water Code of the Russian Federation, adopted on 16 November 1995, provides in Article 111:

> "With a view to maintaining water bodies in the State that meet the ecological requirements for preventing pollution and exhaustion of surface waters, as well as for protecting the habitat of wildlife and plant life, water protection areas shall be established. A water protection area is an area that adjoins a water body and where a special regime of use and protection of natural resources and economic activities shall be established. Within the water protection areas, special defence zones shall be delineated. Within such defence zones it is prohibited to plough land, to cut forests, to place stock-raising farms and camps, and other activities except as provided by the present code".

In the Russian Federation, several Acts determine the policy of sustainable development within which the issues of preserving biological and landscape diversity are decided.

It is worth mentioning the "Main Provisions of the State Strategy of the Russian Federation on Environmental Protection and Sustainable Development", as approved by the Presidential Decree of 4 February 1994, which serves as a basis for constructive interaction between the federal agencies and the agencies of the member-units of the Russian Federation. The principal provisions of the Decree stipulate that the state agencies should ensure the ecologically well grounded placing and development of industrial and agricultural enterprises, towns and other settlements, recreational zones and so forth, as well as ensuring the rehabilitation of degraded areas and the preservation of traditional landscapes.

In 1996, the "Concept of Transit of the Russian Federation to Sustainable Development" was approved. This instrument is oriented on long-term application. It encompasses landscape protection issues and protection of nature.

In addition, it is widely practised in CIS countries to adopt long-term programmes, including programmes for supporting specially protected areas, zapovedniks and national parks, protection of ecosystems of basins of large rivers and lakes, areas of national significance and protection of natural World Heritage sites. In Russia we have a number of remarkable places listed as world natural heritage such as: Lake Baikal, the Komi Forests and the Kamchatka Volcanoes.

There have been several seminars and colloquiums on the themes of the Pan-European Biological and Landscape Strategy. Even though these international events certainly had their own specific objectives, they have also contributed to increasing public awareness.

The Pan-European Biological and Landscape Diversity Strategy attracted the attention of NGOs, some of which have joined forces in the creation of the "Expert Committee for the Protection of Biodiversity of Eastern Europe and Northern Asia". Its membership includes representatives from Moscow, St. Petersburg, Nizhny Novgorod, Samara, Kiev, Ashhabad, Dushanbe, and Berezinsky state zapovednik in Belarus. Through cooperation of all interested experts and organisations in the region, its objective is the preparation of a Regional Action Plan, in compliance with the Pan-European Biological and Landscape Diversity Strategy. It intends to adapt the Strategy to local and regional conditions, to assist in setting general priorities for the whole environmental community of Eastern Europe and Northern Asia and to determine positions and tasks in relation to global and European international processes. NGOs' experts have already begun to analyse the Strategy and to develop scientific approaches to its Action Themes through a research project called "Vision from the East".

The biggest difficulty for the implementation of the Pan-European Biological and Landscape Diversity Strategy is to gain the interest and support of the population and the relevant authorities. At present, the CIS countries are undergoing a serious crisis and conditions are not favourable to environmental protection issues. Faced with the transitional state of the economy, the impoverishment of the population, the disappointment of the people in the so-called democracy, the rise in crime and fall of morals, state authorities do not consider environmental issues as a priority and the annual financial allocations to environmental protection have been reduced. Therefore, there is not enough financial support from federal and local authorities for environmental protection activities.

In Russia, about 40% of the population lives under the poverty line. These people are not interested in the protection of nature. Another 10% of the population include extremely rich people who got their wealth mostly through criminal activities, and corrupt officials who are mainly concerned with further, unpunished plundering of natural resources. They acquire land for construction of luxurious houses or estates, in order to recycle the money obtained through illegal activities.

In between these two extremes the rest of the population lives under conditions of permanent instability. People lack the financial resources and the time for participating in environmental protection activities.

This reality of our social conditions does not allow us to hope for an early implementation of the Pan-European Biological and Landscape Diversity Strategy. But nevertheless, on the positive side we have done much in the way of developing public awareness and the interest of relevant non-governmental organisations. A number of public groups have already established special public organisations committed to implementing the Pan-European Biological and Landscape Diversity Strategy, they have already established a special committee, analysed the situation and expressed an opinion through the special project "Vision from the East".

Finally, it may take us several years to make progress in implementing the Pan-European Biological and Landscape Diversity Strategy but we are determined to do so and we will undertake all the necessary efforts to make it happen.

DISCUSSION

Elisabeth Hopkins

I would just like to take up one point that Professor Kolbasov raised and one very quick comment.

Professor Kolbasov said that 40% of the population lives under the poverty line in the Russian Federation and is therefore not interested in conservation. I have also seen figures showing that about 50 to 60 % of the diet of poor people comes from their own gardens in the country. I personally question whether this kind of division between poverty and conservation is realistic. This topic has been at the centre of discussions in IUCN for years. The concept of landscape can be another instrument in our armoury against this kind of division, which I think is not realistic. Finally, Mr. Chairman, I think that the publication Professor Kolbasov referred to, "Vision from the East", was distributed at Aarhus by Russian NGOs, with the subtitle: "A guide for Children and Ministers".

Oleg Kolbasov

In principle I agree with your remarks, but I would like to expand on my explanations and I can show you a newly published book entitled "Biodiversity Considerations in Russia". This book is very useful, it practically summarises the activities devoted to the Biodiversity Convention; yet officials from the Committee on Environmental Protection of the Russian Federation have told me that there is no money available to pay postage expenses for wide distribution. Maybe there is a special budget devoted to ministers and children. I have a copy of this publication which is very interesting and I hope that it will influence high level officials who deal with landscape and biological diversity protection.

Adrian Phillips

I would like to respond particularly to Liz Hopkin's comments and say at once that I think the emphasis she put on integration between Action Theme 4 and the proposed European Landscape Convention is absolutely right. Indeed, if there isn't integration and a mutual understanding, there will be confusion amongst the people we are trying to talk to. At present, there is some difficulty in understanding how the roles of the bodies associated with Action Theme 4 or with the Convention will cooperate. I think it would be very good if this colloquium was to send some form of message to the two organisations concerned: the Council of Europe, particularly the Congress of Local and Regional Authorities and the European Centre for Nature Conservation (ECNC), to collaborate more closely. Indeed, I believe there are some good indications that this may be about to happen. In my view, if the Convention was in place, it could be seen as the overarching piece of architecture for a lot of work under the Action Theme 4. Indeed, it would give Action Theme 4 a kind of political impact and standing which it currently does not have and conversely, it would give the Convention a far broader base of technical expertise than it can currently muster. Therefore, I think it would be mutually excellent if this could be done.

I would just make one point in relation to Liz's remark that it is important that there should be a strong connection with the people of Europe in this work. I would emphasise that while a convention is very much a top-down instrument in its nature, the origin of this initiative is more bottom-up as it has come up through the Congress of Local and Regional Authorities of Europe. Also, as Jérôme Fromageau and I have tried to explain, the Draft Convention is very much people based. It is not a theoretical top-down structure that we are talking about but the better identification, protection and celebration of the landscape in which everybody lives in Europe.

M. Jean Cabanel, Ministère de l'équipement, des transports et du logement, France

J'ai occupé durant plusieurs années des responsabilités en matière de paysage au Ministère de l'Environnement en France. J'ai le souvenir qu'un projet de directive avait été élaboré à l'initiative de la Fédération Internationale des Architectes-Paysagistes pour l'Europe (EFLA). Cette initiative visait à établir des règles communes en matière de formation et d'exercice de la profession d'architecte-paysagiste. Je n'ai pas retrouvé trace de cette préoccupation dans le projet de convention qui a été présenté. Pourtant, cela aurait été utile dans le contexte de développement des échanges intra-communautaires.

D'autres part, les projets de paysages ont des caractères spécifiques: ils doivent présenter l'évolution des végétaux dans le temps, comporter un plan de gestion, préciser la responsabilité du concepteur (l'architecte-paysagiste en général) dans la mise en oeuvre de ce plan de gestion. Pourtant, malgré ces caractéristiques, les concours de projets paysagers sont lancés selon les mêmes modalités que les projets architecturaux. La "directive services" (directive 92/50 CEE du 18 juin 1992) qui s'applique en particulier aux services "d'architecture paysagère" ne tient pas compte de cette spécificité. Le projet de convention européenne sur le paysage pourrait constituer une opportunité pour pallier cette lacune.

Enfin, et j'en aurai terminé, certaines composantes des paysages sont essentielles, car elles conditionnent la création, le fonctionnement, la qualification des entités paysagères. Il s'agit des structures paysagères qui assurent un rôle déterminant dans la composition et l'échelle des espaces.

A cette notion, qui a été introduite dans la loi française sur le paysage, correspondent concrètement les systèmes hydrauliques, agronomiques, économiques... que constituent les bocages, les terrasses de culture, les vallées et rivières, les zones humides, les forêts... ils donnent des clés de compréhension pour intervenir de manière pertinente sur les espaces. Par exemple, un seul fossé peut perturber l'ensemble d'un site bocager si l'aménageur n'a pas pris en compte son système de fonctionnement global pour le supprimer. Il me parait qu'une telle approche, qui tient compte de la dynamique des systèmes paysagers, aurait pu être introduite avec intérêt dans le projet.

Roger Clark, Countryside Commission, United Kingdom

I would like to add some remarks in relation to landscape structure, the topic raised by the previous speaker, M. J. Cabanel.

I think that the European Landscape Convention is extremely important but it will take some time before it becomes operational. The Pan-European Biological and Landscape Diversity Strategy (PBLDS) is also important, because it already exists and constitutes a practical means of tackling landscape issues. One of the initiatives being taken under Action Theme 4 of PBLDS is to organise a seminar, at a European scale, we hope next Spring, with the European Centre for Nature Conservation, the Countryside Commission, English Nature in England and, we hope, one or two other partners, to look at the issue of landscape structure that has just been mentioned, that is: how can we understand the character of landscape in different parts of Europe; and what are the approaches or the systems being used by national and regional governments in France, in England and other countries, to understand landscape. I am doubtful as to whether it is possible to devise a single system that would apply across Europe but, at a national scale, there clearly is already a lot of interesting work.

The proposed seminar would also look at how such an understanding of landscape can be applied in the main sectors of policy such as spatial planning or the agricultural sector. Therefore, if anybody is interested in this particular proposal for a seminar at a European level next Spring, I would be very happy to speak to them and provide further information.

PART II

COMPARATIVE LAW

Session chaired by Dr. Parvez Hassan, former Chair, IUCN Commission on Environmental Law

Introduction of the Session Chair by Nicholas A. Robinson

It is my pleasure to introduce to you Dr. Parvez Hassan, who is a very well known lawyer in the firm of Hassan & Hassan in Lahore, Pakistan. He is the advocate who has won the most important cases in the High Court and the Supreme Court of Pakistan for the protection of park areas that were about to be developed by mining and other interests. He has also been the lawyer responsible for articulating the decision involving the interpretation of the Constitution of Pakistan which provides that there is a right to a healthy environment. It is a very important precedent for international, comparative, constitutional law. A number of countries have found that there is a fundamental right to the environment in the constitution but Dr. Hassan has taken what might have seemed a difficult case, involving electromagnetic fields, to make this point, and he has done so admirably.

Recently Dr. Hassan has had a very important role within IUCN: he was the chairman of the Statutes Review Committee, a role which I think we should commemorate on the occasion of this 50th anniversary. This Committee had to take the Statutes of IUCN, which were first adopted in 1948, and walk them through a modern process, a process that required consultation with the seventy-four sovereign States and the several hundred non-governmental organisations, which comprise IUCN. He did this with such care, travelling around the world, actually sacrificing his own private law practice so that IUCN could have a firm juridical basis for the next fifty years. I would like to remark on his significant contribution which has cemented the foundation of the first fifty years of IUCN; in honour of his work and on behalf of the Commission of Environmental Law of IUCN we have prepared a leather bound edition of the Statutes in the three languages of IUCN: French, Spanish and English and I wish to present these to him at the opening of this session.

Introductory Remarks by the Chairman

Thank you for this generous introduction, Nick. I welcome all of you to the afternoon session of the Colloquium on Landscape Conservation Law, one of the events organised to celebrate the 50th anniversary of IUCN.

Nick has introduced me as a lawyer from Pakistan. But wherever I travelled internationally, I was always known as Wolfgang Burhenne's successor and now, I am also beginning to be known as Nick Robinson's predecessor. So sandwiched, as I am, between these two legends, it is a privilege and an honour for me to chair this afternoon session.

I would like to make another personal confession on the model of Wolfgang Burhenne's when he talked this morning about how many times he has come to this building and how much he has participated in the work of the legislators. The confession I would like to make is that I am a lawyer, and like most lawyers from developing countries, from the sub-continent of India, Pakistan and Bangladesh, I had to bend to the tradition that all lawyers go into politics. Like Jinnah, Gandhi, Nehru and many others, those who are perceived as having done well in law are expected to take to politics. So I also went down the beaten path. However, when the French Ambassador came to call on me last week in connection with my role as a politician in Pakistan, I had to confess that I had tried hard, on two occasions, to be elected to the Parliament of my country, but that the people of Pakistan had consistently voted to reject my party and my candidature. But, as you can see, what I could not achieve in the National Assembly of the Parliament of Pakistan I seem to be doing here, chairing this important colloquium in this famous building of the Senate of France. So let me express my special gratitude for this privilege which my country has not given me so far.

Anniversaries are great events. Birthdays in personal lives and institutions are edifying experiences, particularly the 50th anniversary of an institution that has done so well over the past five decades. It is a great moment for all those who have taken part in the work of IUCN, who have contributed to its achievements. On this solemn occasion of its 50th anniversary I feel that it is a great privilege to be part of the IUCN family and to be given the opportunity to participate in the celebrations. Françoise Burhenne-Guilmin spoke this morning, quite eloquently, about how the vision was crafted fifty years ago and of how IUCN has grown to become a major, significant player on the international arena for conservation and sustainable development. I would like to felicitate the sponsors, Jérôme Fromageau, Adrian Phillips and my colleague, Nick Robinson, on their enlightened choice of this colloquium for commemorating the 50th anniversary of IUCN.

The morning session focused on the Draft European Landscape Convention and international law. While listening to this morning's presentations and discussions, I felt, with a sense of prophecy, that history may be repeating itself. I felt that the kind of leadership that Europe is providing today, in the field of landscape conservation, is very similar to the leadership Europe provided, many decades ago, in the field of human rights. When the United Nations started work on human rights, and even after the adoption of the Universal Declaration of Human Rights, in 1948, many States were still hesitant about translating that particular concept into a binding treaty. It was Europe that picked up the initiative in the 1950s and came out with the European Convention of Human Rights which was to become a beacon of light for regional arrangements in the Americas, in Africa and is inspiring the kind of arrangements that we are still endeavouring to make in Asia. So I really hope that the work that is being done in connection with the European Landscape Convention may become a model, not only for regional experiences in Asia, Africa, and the other continents, but also for national laws.

In this afternoon session, we will be discussing the comparative law dynamics of landscape conservation. Comparative law is about identifying both the commonalities of national experiences in pursuing the same objective and the same goals, and the differences that may justify separate approaches in certain areas, due to specific historical, geographical, social or economic conditions. This is the type of experience the lawyers, from developed and developing countries, present here today, have in common. When Adrian Phillips spoke this morning, he could have been talking about any legal system or any region, the three important elements in the development of landscape conservation law in Europe which he identified are applicable to any region of the world. He identified first development needs: the pressure for development, the demands for industrialisation, the demands for economic activity; secondly he mentioned abandonment and neglect and, finally, pollution and misuse, as the three major constraining influences diminishing the quality of landscapes.

The same issues are having the same negative effects on landscapes throughout the world and are common to all societies, whether developed or developing. Coming from a developing country, if I had to identify conditioning factors in Pakistan, I would have to pick the same three areas: there is development need in Pakistan, there is abandonment and neglect, and there is pollution and misuse. These we have in common, but for developing countries I would add three additional factors which may not necessarily apply to Europe. The first is population pressure, this is not a problem in Europe but in Asia and some other developing regions there is a horrendous, escalating population pressure rise. When you come from societies, like I do, with a population of 140 million people, with an annual increase rate in excess of 2.5%, you begin to understand the extent of the problem: more people, more needs, more cutting into traditional uses of agriculture, more pressure on cities, more pressure on agriculture.

The second issue is that of poverty; Liz Hopkins felt that we should not really bring this into the debate. I agree, it may not be quite appropriate, but it is the harsh reality that where there is poverty, society cannot really afford the luxury of the kind of exercise that we are going through. I agree with Liz when she says that poverty should not be an issue in our commitment, but on the ground, the essential reality is that it is an issue. Again, speaking from national experience: in Pakistan, we have a fairly significant rate of growth but that growth pattern merely signifies that the rich keep getting richer, and the poor keep getting poorer. On balance the country may have done well, but the poor are more marginalised than they were yesterday. And particularly, when a country in South Asia chooses the nuclear option with the sanctions imposed against it as a consequence, then the difference in the national pattern of growth is that the poor keep getting poorer and the rich are also becoming poor. As you have guessed this is the situation in Pakistan and India, both subjected to economic sanctions because of the nuclear option they, unfortunately, have chosen.

The third factor, specific to developing countries, is the resource constraint. I needn't go into it to a great extent as it is quite well known.

What is important is that the objectives are the same in developed and developing countries. There is the same sensitivity to landscape planning, management, and aesthetics. I need only to remind you of the Moguls, in the sub-continent of India and Pakistan; not only did they build magnificent famous monuments like the Taj Mahal, the Shalamar Gardens and the great Mosques at Lahore and Delhi, they also had a great sensitivity to aesthetics and to landscape planning. Those societies were rich because of their landscape sensitivity and their traditions were passed down to us. To say that poverty suppresses or curbs aesthetic sense is wrong: the senses are there, it is just a matter of priorities and economic issues.

With this introductory comment I merely wanted to highlight the commonality in the experience of developed and developing countries. There is an important common commitment which is to facilitate interaction between people and nature. As Adrian Phillips pointed out earlier: "we have to manage the process of change". Three elements emerged from this morning's session which can serve as guidelines for legislation, both national and regional: the process of change has to be underpinned by public participation, public awareness, and a system of incentives.

To discuss all these issues we have a very distinguished panel of speakers. I take particular pleasure in pointing out that this is a panel comprising colleagues I have worked with over the years, I am happy that they have found time to be here. We will travel with them, in a comparative law assessment, from Singapore to North America, to the European landscape and to Africa. Not all the systems are represented, but I think that the various presentations will give us a fairly good idea of the comparative law issues which might emerge from this debate.

To begin, I would like to introduce Koh Kheng Lian to speak about Singapore and its system. Koh Kheng Lian is Vice Chair of the IUCN Commission on Environmental Law, but I look at her more as "Ms. Capacity Builder". In my incarnation as former Chairman of the Commission on Environmental Law of IUCN, when we developed a project in Singapore, called the Asia Pacific Centre for Environmental Law, I went hunting for a venue, funds, commitments, vitality, charisma and energy, I found all those in Koh Kheng Lian. The result being that, with the commitment and the support we gave her, she is now the Director of APCEL, the Asia Pacific Centre for Environmental Law, in Singapore.

Singapore: Fashioning Landscape for "The Garden City"

Koh Kheng Lian, *Vice Chair, IUCN Commission on Environmental Law; Professor, Faculty of Law, National University of Singapore*

I would first like to thank the organisers for arranging this very important colloquium, in this august building, where I'll take great pleasure in talking to you about Singapore, the garden city where I come from.

The Garden City of Singapore will unfold itself to the foreign visitor the moment he steps into the Singapore Changi International Airport. Greeted by festoons of plants and flowers, albeit some artificial, the visitor is feasted with a garden landscape, both indoors and outdoors. The drive down the city is greeted with more cultivated greenery – well kept trees, shrubs, flowers, and creepers at overhead bridges. And, if he happens to visit a high rise apartment – in an urban city of mainly high rise apartment buildings – he may also find a "skyrise garden" with neighbourhood parks and gardens.

The tiny urban industrial city of some 647.5 square kilometres, with a population of 3.6 million is well known as a *Cité Jardin*. Despite the rapid industrialisation, since the 1960s, when a great part of the natural surroundings, namely: nature reserves, forests, mangroves, flora, fauna had to disappear to make way for infrastructures, industrial and urban centres, Singapore has emerged relatively unscathed by negative environmental impacts. David Bellamy, a well-known conserva-tionist, said that Singapore "is a role model for other cities in sustainable development".[14] Alexandra A. Seno, writing in the 5 December 1997 issue of Asiaweek said: "With its landscaped grounds and profusion of greenery, Singapore well deserves the "Garden City" title".

Whose brainchild was the Garden City? Was it just a physical concept or did it go further? It was the brainchild of Singapore's "architect", the former Prime Minister, Lee Kuan Yew, now Senior Minister (SM). There were two main reasons for the Senior Minister's passion for gardens. First, to woo investors – "In wooing investors, even the trees matter", so he said on 1 August 1996 when the Economic Development Board of Singapore celebrated its 35th Anniversary. He thought that well-kept trees and gardens were a subtle way of convincing potential investors, in the early crucial years, that Singapore was an efficient and effective place. That was during the start of Singapore's transformation, in the 1960s, from an entrepôt port into the industrial city it is today. When the bulldozers started to work clearing land, mangroves, reclaiming marshes and wetlands, the Garden City was slowly being developed. The very first sentence of the Introduction to the book, "Lee Kuan Yew: The Man and his Ideas"[15] says: "Lee Kuan Yew wanted Singapore to become a garden city, to soften the harshness of life in one of the world's most densely populated countries..."

The verdant city of Singapore today is the result of a deliberate 30 years of policy which, according to the Senior Minister, required "political will and sustained effort". Speaking at the official opening of the new, $5 million National Orchid Garden, at the Singapore Botanic Gardens, on 20th October 1995 he said: "I have always believed that a blighted urban landscape, a concrete jungl,e destroys the human spirit. We need the greenery of nature to lift up our spirits".

This morning we heard about the interaction between man and nature; the spiritual attributes of human beings depend on this interaction. Lee Kuan Yew, as you may know, was a graduate from Cambridge, where he read law and was very inspired by the beauty of the English countryside. He was inspired by the British botanical gardens. He travelled extensively, visited India, Pakistan and other countries but he said: "One thing that struck me in my travels was the way in which the British, systematically, created botanical gardens wherever they created huge settlements".

So it was that in the 1960s the trees did woo many investors. And it appears that in 1963, when the concept of sustainable development had not yet gained political legitimacy, the then Prime Minister sowed the seed of the Garden City by launching the annual tree-planting campaigns, replaced by the "Clean and Green Week " in 1990.

So important is this concept of the garden city to Singapore that, in 1968, during the second reading of the Environmental Public Health Bill, it was stated: "The improvement in the quality of our urban environment and the transformation of Singapore into a garden city – a clean and green city – is the declared objective of the government". Where else in the world do you have the declaration of a garden city being made in Parliament? 1968 was the high water mark of Singapore's industrialisation and urbanisation. Some of the highly polluting industries were and are chemical,

---

[14] *The Straits Times*, 4 May 1993.

[15] Han Fook Kwang, Warren Fernandez, Sumiko Tan, 1997.

petro-chemical industries, oil refineries, gas, electrical and electronic industries as well as shipping and ship-repairing. The above declaration was an attempt to integrate environment and economic development – a clean and green industrial city. This was part of Singapore's brand of sustainable development. Its land use planning and pollution laws ensure a clean and pollution-free environment. Its laws relating to tree planting and conservation of flora and fauna have, on the whole, created the *Cité Jardin* after over 30 years.

The Lee Kuan Yew concept of *Cité Jardin de Singapour* was further enhanced and developed by the second echelon of leaders. When the present Prime Minister Goh Chok Tong took over from Lee Kuan Yew, in 1991, he had already, as First Deputy Prime Minister, launched the first Clean and Green Week in November 1990. This coincided with the 20th Tree Planting Day. At the time, he stated that this marked a shift in emphasis, from just the greening and cleaning of Singapore, to a total approach in shaping and changing attitudes towards the environment. He said: "We want an environment that enchants us .... we should adopt a total approach towards the environment. Every aspect must be made beautiful and everyone must play his part".

Describing the Clean and Green Week as a continuation of past efforts he further said: "It marks a new phase in our aspiration to make Singapore the most enchanting equatorial city-state, a city within a park".[16] The concept is that of a garden within a garden, like the orchid garden in the botanic gardens. The National Parks of Singapore organises exhibitions to encourage people to create gardens in their apartments in high rise buildings, or even on top of the buildings. This concept is borderless, from a garden in the countryside to a garden in your own home.

In the area of environment nothing succeeds like having a political will to do something. I have gone into an *excursus* of the political will of two generations of leaders, since Singapore gained independence in 1963, to make Singapore a Garden City. But we owe its success to its progenitor, Mr. Lee Kuan Yew, without whose ideas, vision and willpower Singapore might today be a blighted, concrete, industrial city, as many such industrial cities in other parts of the world have become.

How did Singapore turn into the urban garden landscape that it is today? What are the landscape conservation laws necessary to bring this about?

According to "The Shorter Oxford English Dictionary" a "garden city" is "a real estate development combining the advantages of town and country life, providing open spaces and garden plots". The word "garden" itself is defined as an "enclosed plot or ground devoted to the cultivation of flowers, fruits and vegetables. Ornamental grounds used as a place of public resort" Singapore's Garden City goes far beyond this concept.

Singapore inherited from its British colonial masters a system of land use and planning control. Some of the laws governing planning and control (hard and soft laws) are: the Planning Act, the Building Control Act, the National Parks Act, the Master Plan (as revised by the Concept Plan of 1971), the Revised Concept Plan 1991 (which included a "Green and Blue Plan"), the Singapore Green Plan Action Programme and the Recommendations of the Singapore Green Plan Workgroup 5 on Nature Conservation, of March 1993. A combination of these hard and soft laws has been used to fashion Singapore as a garden city.

The achievement of the various laws including the various "Green Plans" was to fashion Singapore's garden landscape. Zoning is used as a planning device to regulate the location of various uses of land so as to ensure that similar and compatible uses are located together while conflicting uses are located as far apart as possible.[17] The Master Plan together with the Concept

---

[16] *The Straits Times*, 5 November 1990.

[17] Environmental Protection in Singapore: A handbook, 2-3.

Plan and the Revised Concept Plan take into consideration environmental aspects like pollution and the need for a clean and green environment. Thus, for example, as Singapore was poised for industrialisation, land use was zoned with a view of segregating water catchment areas and residential areas from polluting industries. The approach to land use was at two levels – the macro and micro level. Thus, there are provisions for buffer zones of green spaces and gardens even within industrial estates.

The dilemma which Singapore, more than any other country in the world, has faced is to find the balance between development and maintaining an urban landscape of natural and cultivated greenery and a sustainable ecosystem, in a very limited space of 647.5 square kilometres, with a growing population of 3.6 million. The approach, therefore, had to be pragmatic. This strategy has led to a number of mistakes.

Under the Green Plan, 5% of the land of Singapore is set aside for nature conservation, with 19 nature areas incorporated into the Revised Concept Plan 1991. However, only 3 of the 19 areas are protected by legislation, namely: the Botanic Gardens, the Fort Canning Park and the Bukit Timah Nature Reserves. Others cover forest areas, mangrove swamps, ridges and offshore islands which are rich in flora and fauna. These areas are to be incorporated into the Development Guide Plans (DGPs) of the Concept Plan (under the Green and Blue Plan). To connect all the 19 nature sites, there will be a Park Connectors Network, a "tapestry of Green" linking all of them. The pragmatic approach is to enable recreational use, so there will be bicycle tracts for the public to enjoy and have access to nature and wildlife.

To support and supplement the natural areas, some of which have been reduced by industrialisation, numerous trees have been planted to line Singapore's streets and parks. Indeed, since 1970 more than five million trees and shrubs have been planted along major roads and streets. The tree planting policy was stated in Singapore's National Report for the 1992 United Nations Conference on Environment and Development Preparatory Committee: "From the outset, Singapore has always recognised the role of plant cover in alleviating pollution, promoting rainfall and in improving the aesthetic quality of life, ..." this is yet another illustration of pragmatic Singapore. At this juncture, the rationale of urban tree planting and conservation is: "trees woo investors, trees are an integral part of a garden which lifts the soul and give a quality of life, trees make rain...".

In the 1960s and 1970s when Singapore, which was separated from Malaysia in 1965, engaged in heavy industrialisation for its economic survival, it was a crucial moment in Singapore's economic development. As some of the natural areas were bulldozed and land was reclaimed from its wetlands, the vision of the Garden City was, at times, compromised but not lost. In the 1970s the Government continued its efforts to develop Singapore into a garden city and to provide recreational activities for a growing urban population. In 1970, the Trees and Plants Act (Preservation and Improvement of Amenities) was passed, with the objective of ensuring the preservation and growing of trees and plants. It restricted the felling and cutting of trees exceeding five feet in girth. The Act was subsequently amended and consolidated in the Parks and Trees Act, 1975. This Act was aimed at developing, protecting and regulating public parks and gardens and at planting and preserving trees. The main objective was to strengthen the institutional framework – it consolidated the Botanic Gardens Act and Section 7 Part V of the Local Government Integration Act. A Commissioner of Parks and Recreation and other Deputy and Assistant Commissioners were appointed in order to enhance planning and management of gardens and public parks.

On the substantive side, the Act restricts the felling and cutting of trees with a girth exceeding one metre, measured half a metre from the ground, growing on any vacant land not developed for residential or industrial purposes. Permission must be obtained from the Commissioner for felling such trees. The Act also empowered the Commissioner to require the occupier/owner of vacant land to plant trees and to maintain them. It also empowers the Commissioner to compel the planting of trees and plants around a building.

The next flourishing stage came in the late 1980s when Singapore had achieved economic growth. The Garden City was further developed with the passing of the National Parks Act 1990 (NPA). It raised the status of the Botanic Gardens and Fort Canning Park to National Parks. The government had approved a $51 million development programme to make the Botanic Gardens a leading institution for equatorial botany and horticulture and also to create an outstanding educational and recreational garden. The run-down Fort Canning Park was given S$25 million to redevelop into a recreational and cultural park. The Bukit Timah Nature Reserve was to be developed to its full potential. Speaking at the second reading of the National Parks Bill on 29 March 1990, the then Minister for National Development said:

> "Singapore is a city-state. It is easy to let the urban sprawl encroach into our green and open spaces. The formation of the National Parks Board is our commitment to conserve our national heritage. It is also another step towards improving the quality of life of the present and future generation of Singaporeans".

Speaking of present and future generations underlines the concept of sustainable development in an urban context – a quality of life among clean and green surroundings. Armed with more teeth and wherewithal, both the new National Parks Board and the Parks and Recreation Department (PRD) further developed Singapore's greenery. With the desire to take the garden city one step further to be a model and keeping pace with Singaporeans' rising expectations, the two organisations merged into a new body, becoming, in July 1996, the National Parks Board under The National Parks Act 1996. Nparks, as it is now known, is the Government Agency for the management and maintenance of the green areas. It has a staff of 591 permanent members and 468 day labourers. In 1997 the operating expenditure was S$79,300,00, with an additional S$31,168,190.00 for development projects. Their mission statement is: "We make Singapore our Garden".[18]

NParks enjoys more autonomy and has taken some new directions. In his statement, Tan Keong Choon, Chairman of the National Parks Board,[19] outlined the new directions:

> "Nparks aspires to actively manage our parks and greenery ... This translates into developing green areas for ... recreational and leisure needs, to promote social interaction, encouraging a sense of ownership and bringing the Garden to the doorstep of everyone's home. ... We must expand our vision of Singapore as a garden city".

This expansion of the vision of Singapore as a garden city is mainly spelt out in the functions of the Nparks Board under section 6 of the National Parks Act 1996 (some of which were in the predecessor legislation for example, the 1990 National Parks Act). The functional features of the garden city involve a symbiosis of mankind, nature and landscape whether natural or cultivated. Article 6 of the 1996 National Parks Act captures the values of nature in listing the functions of the NParks Board:

- "to propagate, protect and preserve the plants and animals of Singapore ... to preserve objects and places of aesthetic, historical or scientific interest;"

- "to provide and control facilities for the study of and research into matters relating to animals and plants;"

- "to exhibit objects illustrative of the life sciences, applied sciences, history, technology and industry;"

---

[18] Gardenwise, The Newsletter of the Singapore Botanic Gardens, Vol. IX, July 1997.

[19] Annual Report 1996/97.

- "to promote the study, research and dissemination of knowledge in botany, horticulture, biotechnology, arboriculture, landscape architecture, parks and recreational management and natural and local history;"

- "to provide, manage and promote recreational, cultural, historical, research and educational facilities and resources in national parks, nature reserves and parklands and encourage their full and proper use by members of the public."

The elements that are behind fashioning Singapore's greenery include aesthetic, historical, scientific, recreational, educational, research and also economic interests.

Singapore has little by way of great landscapes, as contemplated by the European Landscape Convention – for example, huge farmlands near mountains and lakes have created a distinctive feature in parts of rural Europe. A comparable type of landscape would be Singapore's last vestige of a Malay fishing village in an island off Singapore – Pulau Ubin. In mainland Singapore, some of the landscapes, greenery and nature areas have to be rebuilt or fashioned where none existed before. For example, the Chinese Garden, in classical, Northern Chinese, imperial architectural style, serves as a theme park. Fort Canning Park, as we shall see later, preserves some historical heritage of the first botanical garden, with crops and spices being experimented for export. There is also the Japanese Garden which depicts one of the most beautiful miniature landscape Gardens in the East. It has a place in Singapore's Garden City not only for its beauty but also as a symbol of the role played by Japanese investors in the early years of Singapore's industrial development. In addition, there is the Jurong Birdpark, the largest in the world, featuring the world's tallest man-made waterfall. Practically devoid of wildlife, urban Singapore has a zoo and offers a night safari with nocturnal creatures in a zoo environment reminiscent of a wildlife park.

Let us look briefly at how the law (hard and soft) further accelerated the enhancement and concept of the Garden City in the 1990s.

The first 22 years, since the 1968 declaration made in Parliament to develop the Garden City, saw mainly the maintenance and provision of gardens, parks and open spaces. Many trees were planted along the roads. Provision was also made for recreational facilities in order to utilise the "green" places.

From 1990 onwards a new direction was mapped out in "Living the Next Lap –Towards a Tropical City of Excellence" (1992). The Revised Concept Plan of 1991 took another step forward by stating:

> "Our intention is to further shape our environment with greenery and waterways. We should help landscape a Singapore so intertwined with tropical greenery that it gives the illusion of being a city that has sprung out of a garden. We also want to heighten the feeling of island living. More access to the water which laps our shores e.g. Marina Bay. The use of rivers and waterways can also help to create an image of islands within an island. The greening of the city will create the sense of gardens within a garden."

The framework to achieve these objectives was the Green and Blue Plan which comprises the following:

- natural open spaces – such as mangrove swamps, wooded areas and nature reserves;
- major parks and gardens – such as regional parks and district parks;
- sports and recreation grounds;
- boundary separations – which serve as green linkages connecting major parks and recreational areas as green belts between urbanised districts;
- internal greenways and connectors – greenways can be naturally landscaped or informal;
- other open areas;
- waterways, like the Singapore river, the other rivers, and major canals.

Thus, from 1990 onwards, the concept of the garden became clearer. Some of its highlights and achievements are:

- Improvement of the landscape – landscapes along the roadsides are enhanced with colourful plants and shrubs. In 1995, for example, about 5,400 flowering trees and 210,600 colourful flowering shrubs were added to road junctions, expressway interchanges and roadside gardens. Some 7,800 palms and trees were planted in housing estates. There is also a programme for vacant state land.

- The 1990s saw further efforts at tree conservation. On 2 August 1991 a policy for tree conservation singled out two areas, namely: the Central part of Singapore and the Changi area where all trees with a girth size of more than one metre, measured half-a-meter above the ground, would no longer be cut without prior authorisation.

- As new construction works for buildings and roads erode green areas, private developers and other bodies like the Land Transport Authority are required to plant trees and provide green open spaces in their residential, commercial and industrial projects.

- According to the Annual Report 1995/96 of the Parks and Recreation Department, there were 28 regional parks, 166 community parks, 35 city parks and 4 park connector networks. There are plans for more: there should be 14 park connectors, covering some 40 km, by the year 2000.

Let us look at some of the major gardens and parks:

- Botanic Gardens: in 1989, at the 130th Anniversary of the Botanic Gardens, a Master-Plan was announced to develop the gardens as a leading tropical institution for botany and horticulture. The garden was also to be upgraded to feature different varieties of plants. Today these goals have been achieved. To attract more visitors and to bring musical life to the garden, a Symphony Performance Shell was constructed as the Symphony Lake of the island. There are now weekend musical performances. Another significant development of the 1990s is the S$5 million National Orchid Garden housed in the Botanic Gardens, officially opened by SM Lee Kuan Yew in October 1995. The Gardens continue to enhance the Garden City Programme, becoming a resource centre in the region for horticulture and to build capacity on landscape planting, botany and nature appreciation.

- Fort Canning Park: one of the two National Parks, it was very downgraded some years ago, but it has been given more than a face lift. It has a historical setting that goes back to the 14th Century, when it was the seat of the Malay Kingdom, Temasek. Sir Stamford Raffles, who founded Singapore in 1819, established the first botanical garden here in 1822, where crops like spices, vegetables and other raw materials were grown for potential economic gains. Today, there is a Spice Garden – a replica of the original 19 ha. tract where Raffles established the first "experimental and botanical garden". Situated in the heart of Singapore's Civic and Cultural District, Fort Canning Park serves as a green lung and a cultural heritage site, easily accessible for the office worker.

- Bukit Timah Nature Reserve: its history dates back to 1833 when it was established as a Forest Reserve, and has since been protected by legislation. It has some of the finest variety of plant species, primary and secondary forests. To bring about an interaction between people and nature, amenities such as signage, map boards, pathways, benches and cycling trails have been put up or constructed to encourage the urban dwellers to appreciate and enjoy nature. Like in the other 19 Nature Areas recommended under the Singapore Green Plan – Workgroup 5, Nature Conservation, a reforestation scheme is being conducted in this Nature Reserve.

- Sungei Buloh: situated on the Northwest coast of Singapore, the Sungei Buloh Nature Park, comprising 87 ha. of wetlands, is a stop-over for migratory birds, particularly plovers and sandpipers. It was one of the 19 nature areas which were recognised for conservation, as it has a rich wildlife and beautiful landscape. Officially opened by Prime Minister Goh Chock Tong on 6 December 1993, it was once an area for prawn and fish farms but, in 1989, the farmers were resettled and it was developed into a nature park. It is a nature park within the Garden City, it satisfies all the criteria to be designated as a Ramsar site. However, Singapore has not yet ratified the 1971 Ramsar Convention on Wetlands of International Importance.[20]

Have there been any blots on the garden path? Some areas were, and are, being developed too rapidly, without due consideration given to integrating environment and development. One such example is the Senoko haven for migratory birds. For birds and nature lovers, Senoko, once a marshland where about 190 species of migratory birds used to make their home, is today a home for some 17,000 public-housing dwellers. The appeal by Friends of Senoko, in 1994, to integrate some 76 out of 168 ha. into a larger area for public housing was turned down by the authorities. The group then appealed for only 20 ha. but it was still refused. This, even though the Nature Society of Singapore (an NGO) and the Urban Redevelopment Authority (a statutory board) under the Ministry for National Development had some years earlier designated it as a "nature park" and "bird sanctuary". This would have been an excellent example of the integration of environment and development, called for by global environmental instruments like the Convention on Biological Diversity of 1992 and also the ASEAN Agreement on the Conservation of Nature and Natural Resources (1985).

The fight between "concretising" and leaving nature areas for promoting sustainable development is still ongoing. There has been disquiet over bulldozers and reclamation works or threatened bulldozing and reclamation in some green areas such as wetlands. Perhaps it was not realised that these perform an important ecological function.

Be that as it may, perhaps when the dust has settled and the concrete slabs are embedded in the ground, NParks will find a spot to further fashion another landscape, even though this cannot replace the natural greenery that has disappeared. This is pragmatism! We were recently reminded in an article "Lessons from a Raintree: Battered but not Bowed"[21] that a raintree (as pointed out by a former Parks Commissioner, Wang Yew Kwan) planted 26 years ago looked "dead" or "dying"; he said that the concrete which was used to cover the ground around the tree in 1995 could have affected its intake of water: "keeping the tree alive is no mere environmental issue, but a matter of national symbolism". The article went on to say: "As the first fruit of Singapore's tree planting campaign, the Mount Faber tree is a living monument to a garden city vision and has kept the country from becoming a concrete jungle like many other cities".

A number of voices have been heard in favour of leaving a little natural green and beach around, in the face of more developments for man-made beach resorts and other projects. Singapore aspires to be a model Green City in the year 2000. The countdown to the millennium has started. There is still room for improvement, as there always will be, in all matters. As I was preparing this paper, in my high-rise garden apartment, with natural and artificial plants, I could hear birds chirping outside my window. Surely, this is country living in an urban context!

---

[20] Convention on Wetlands of International Importance Especially as Waterfowl Habitat, 2 February 1971, Ramsar, 11 ILM. 963.

[21] *The Straits Times,* 19 November 1997.

Commentator: *Charles Okidi, Vice Chair, IUCN Commission on Environmental Law; Founding Dean of the School of Environmental Studies of Moi University in Kenya; currently Task Manager for the UNEP/UNDP/Dutch Government joint project in Environmental Law and Institutions*

I am delighted to be here. To comment on the paper just presented by Professor Koh Kheng Lian is not an easy task because it is entirely an exposé of superlatives, so the challenge for me is to either come up with a higher level of superlatives or to come up with contradictions so compelling as to demonstrate that her superlatives were misleading. Unfortunately I am not half as poetic as she is, I can therefore not match her literary eloquence and outdo her superlatives. At the same time I have no compelling contradictions to offer. I had the chance of being in Singapore in June this year and I can testify that the level of cleanliness, the tidiness, the attractiveness of Singapore is what many of us imagine exists only in novels. I saw it in reality. In fact, a lawyer friend from Pakistan, not Parvez, found that Singapore is so clean and so tidy almost to the point of being boring. It is indeed a unique case. One would assume that it is simply due to the disciplined behaviour of the population. Is it just that there is no littering or do official cleaners work all night to restore tidiness before the city wakes up next morning?

However, everyone is aware that Singapore is not only a fine city but also a city of fines; there are penalties for any behaviour that would spoil the environment. I am happy with the array of statutory provisions that Koh Kheng Lian has outlined in her presentation, showing that Singapore has enforceable rules which are, indeed, enforced. But my fear is that as pressure mounts in a given country, some of the statutes get drastically amended and sometimes repealed in order to give some flexibility. This has happened in a number of countries as, for instance, in the USA, where many of the pioneer statutes for environmental protection adopted in the 1970s have suffered this fate. Given the wealth and beauty of Singapore, the strong personality of the Senior Minister helping, I would have hoped for a constitutional entrenchment of these environmental provisions, in order to render amendments more difficult.

My second observation is that with fines yes, discipline can be maintained, but we have also seen that in many places, where liberalisation and so called democratisation take place, there is a tendency for people to rebel against the strict discipline and to strive for more freedom of action. The fines could become a source of protest. Incidentally I was told, last June, that the fines alone fetch up to 5 million dollars per year for the Government revenue. There is efficiency, there is tendency for compliance but I would have liked to hear more comments about the possible scenario if pressure mounts against this quasi-repressive, yet admirable, regime.

I ask myself why weren't there five or six more people like Lee Kuan Yew in the 1960s? Why was he so unique? How did he manage to inculcate that kind of discipline into the people? I wish this could have been the case in Kenya, where I live, as Nairobi, "the green city in the sun" is no longer so green. Where population pressure rises and poverty rises, the people who suffer from neglect of the environment are the poor people. So let no one kid us into believing that the poor people have to live with poverty and filth because that is their destiny.

Finally, the literature on the Asian situation tells us that because of increasing population pressure on agriculture, of the arable land available, 110% is already under cultivation, which means that there are already significant incursions into sensitive areas that should not be cultivated. I admire the beauty of Singapore and I hope that these unfortunate incursions into sensitive areas do not affect it.

North America: Statutory Greenways and Regional Landscape Systems

Nicholas A. Robinson, *Chair, IUCN Commission on Environmental Law; Professor, School of Law, Pace University (USA)*

A new development in North America, which has taken place in the last decade, is the Greenway Movement. From Europe, Asia or Africa it is rather difficult to see beyond the national levels of the Federal Government of the United States or the Federal Government of Canada, but the provinces in Canada and in the USA have substantial authority over land use questions and over the issue of the countryside. A number of programmes have been created in North America to define how to protect these areas.

Most of those who work internationally are familiar with Abraham Lincoln's Order to set aside Yosemite Valley in California as the first large reserve in the USA, or with the designation by Congress of the first national park at Yellowstone in the 1870s, or with the National Parks Service, which was established in the first part of the 20th century. What is less known internationally is what is going on, and has gone on for a hundred years, within the states and provinces. In particular I shall describe the first of the Greenway Movements in the USA which was established by law for the Hudson River Valley.

New York State established its first State Park, which was also the first State Park in the USA, in the late 19th century, at Niagara Falls, which it shares with Ontario in Canada. New York State established the first State Park System in the nation at around the same time and, in 1894, it incorporated into its Constitution the preservation of the Forest Preserve in the Adirondack and Catskill Mountains. This was the first time in legislation that a wild area was required to be maintained wild by law. Article 14 of the New York State Constitution provides that: "the forest preserve shall be kept forever wild forest land". This area is much larger than Yellowstone National Park but, unlike Yellowstone National Park, it has a cultural heritage integrated with a natural heritage. Villages, farms, timberlands and private recreation lands, including the Lake Placid winter Olympics grounds, coexist with wild forests, wetlands, habitats for rare and endangered species, lakes and rivers. Even the privately owned lands, along about 125 miles of undeveloped rivers, are regulated under a State "Wild and Scenic Rivers" Law.

These private lands inside the Adirondack Park are subject to land use and development control that have been established by the Adirondack Park Agency, which is an independent land use authority established by State statute. The Adirondack Park Agency establishes zoning and town and country planning in all of the municipalities that fail to adopt comparable systems of their own. The purpose of all this planning is to ensure that land development by private or public owners of land inside the park will not adversely affect the constitutionally protected, "forever wild", forest lands that are also inside the Park. While the Adirondack example has been completely successful in protecting the wild land and controlling the urban sprawl and development of private land or local government land, it has created an adversarial relationship between the environmentalists outside the park and the State authorities that regulate the park on the one hand, and on the other, the people who live inside the park on private lands and who would rather have greater economic development to enhance their community wealth. The local residents resent the limitations on their economic life. They resent the fact that people outside the municipalities are making decisions for them. They do not wish to be a colony of the rest of New York State. They wish to have their local self-rule, and they resent the fact that they do not have full democracy.

This has influenced how New York State went about creating the next system of land protection and management for landscape. It happened at a time when many people were worried, throughout the USA, and in Provinces like British Columbia in Canada, about the same issues that were described this morning: urban sprawl, housing expansion in the suburbs taking over land that could be protected, closing off landscapes by developments and failing to rehabilitate the urban core in the old industrial areas, the so called "rust belt". These trends led the legislature of New York, and environmental advocates, to explore a more collaborative, less regulatory approach to management of landscape.

In 1991 the New York State legislature enacted the Hudson River Valley Greenway Act. This statute covers the Hudson River Valley from New York City to Saratoga County, above Albany, about 250 kilometres to the North. The Greenway goes right up to the edge of the Adirondack Mountains. The area, and the reasons for the enactment of the statute, as recorded in the statute, are similar to the values that Adrian Phillips chronicled for us this morning:

- This is a region rich in culture and history;
- It is a natural watershed, all of the water in the Hudson River Valley enters the river and empties into the Atlantic;
- The river itself is rich in fish species including sturgeon and striped bass;
- The Hudson was carved by glaciers and, while it is geographically as deep as the Grand Canyon, it has silted up to sea level so that the entire valley is at sea level. Although the salt front only goes as far as 75 miles, the rise and fall of the tides are felt as far as 200 miles into New York State;
- The hills along each side of the valley are quite spectacular, the glacier carved the river through mountains which are about 50 kilometres North of New York, known as the Hudson Highlands.

The renowned German travel guide Baedeker did us the honour of saying that the Hudson River here was finer than the Rhine, something I love to quote. This is where the West Point Military Academy is located and where American revolutionaries forged the chain across the river to prevent the British fleet from controlling the Valley and linking New York City with Canada during the revolution, thereby preventing the management of the entire set of colonies by the British army. Here too is where the American naturalists Burroughs and Osborn inspired the conservation movement in the late 19th century. Here is where the "Hudson River School of American Landscape Painting" was born, the first indigenous American painting genre. Here too is where Washington Irving lived and wrote the first literature by an American that was well regarded in Europe. Here is where Samuel Morse lived and the telegraph was invented and where our President Franklin Roosevelt lived. The Valley itself is a patchwork of villages from old sailing ports founded by New Englanders, who went whaling from a town called Hudson, to the mill towns of the early industrial revolution. There are farm lands throughout the valley. There are resorts, universities, park lands, hunting and fishing grounds and the National Estuary Research Program of our National Oceanic and Atmospheric Administration. It is still a commercial shipping route for cargo ships; container ships go to the port of Albany, well inland, not far from Canada. This is where the Erie Canal begins, which first linked the Hudson across New York to the Great Lakes and opened that area to development.

The danger to this rich landscape over so large an area of the Hudson River Valley arises from inconsistent land use laws adopted by the different municipalities. Each of the local governments would protect one value or another. One town could allow the wrong kind of development right up to the edge of another town which was protecting its landscape from that adverse development. Transportation corridors would cut off the migratory movement of deer and other species. The old and obsolete industrial areas were left to fall apart. Some communities would protect their historic and cultural buildings, their architectural patrimony, while others would bulldoze them. These practices were creating a chaotic ambience for the entire Hudson River Valley; but rather than impose a regulatory land use control system like the one in the Adirondacks, one possible system over this vast area, the New York State legislature chose to create two different management systems.

The first Greenway system adopted is the establishment of the Hudson River Valley Greenways Communities Council, a body representative of the local governments from all over the Valley, with special representation for farmers to give them a chance to develop special economic and tax incentives to keep the farming community alive. The Council is charged with preparing regional plans and studies; it basically creates a technical advisory context for every community to adopt comparable land use laws to protect the same values and themes throughout the Valley. The themes are to be codified in a Hudson River Valley Compact, or formal agreement among all these local governments, so that they can consensually arrive at a common management system for the entire region. The Council commissions studies, derives themes from these studies and is charged by statute to conduct analysis on "scientific, environmental, economic, tourism and cultural studies in the valley".

The second component of this system is the creation of the Hudson River Valley Greenway Heritage Conservancy. The Conservancy is a state chartered corporation, known in our parlance as a Public Benefit Authority. It actually has all the powers of a development authority, but to apply these powers to promote the landscape and not to develop it in adverse ways. For instance, it works to link the Valley's tourism infrastructure, to build sustainable use of cultural and natural heritage. It designates bicycle touring routes and has now designated a long distance bicycle route on both sides of the Valley. It designates a river trail for kayaking and canoeing up and down the entire river, with camping facilities. It is now well along the way to linking all the hiking trails up and down both sides of the Valley. It will be possible to walk from Albany to New York City and back or in any part of the Valley on the touring path and trail. The Greenway Heritage Conservancy promotes the integration of all of the public land, all of the parks and cultural amenities, all of the historic properties, making them mutually accessible; it works with the hunters to ensure that there will still be hunting grounds in the area. It works with the fishermen for the river and the tributaries and it works with the agricultural interests to establish farmer's markets. The Greenway includes urban cultural parks in the old villages and cities, which are beautiful, old, rundown architectural structures. The Conservancy seeks funding from public and private sources to give as grants to stabilise and maintain facades so as to bring back the architecture of the past and keep it alive in the future. It was my privilege to serve as the first chairman of this Conservancy and to organise its statutory rules, to implement it and get it off to a good start. The Greenway Conservancy has been working diligently to build up these mutually supporting systems, economic, scientific, cultural systems, right across the board, for natural and cultural areas uses, compatible with the economic life in the Valley.

I have used this example of the Hudson Valley because it was the first to be adopted by statute, but several other states and provinces have now also adopted similar statutes and the Greenways are criss-crossing North America. These greenways generically are linear corridors of land and water and the cultural, natural and recreational resources that they encompass. For instance, Massachusetts has a 3,005 acre Greenway on a 70-mile stretch of the Connecticut River, encompassing public and private lands, farms, parks, woods lots. There are now 500 Greenways across the United States and Canada. In 1995, in Vancouver, British Columbia, the Vancouver Greenway Plan was adopted. It provides for the preservation of open space, the promotion of pathway systems for pedestrians and cyclists and the enhancement of the flora and fauna in the area. The Greenway developments, spanning several states and provinces, tend to be very similar. The states of Minnesota, Indianapolis, Indiana, Delaware and Oregon have enacted state statutes. The Willamette River Greenway is now producing a comparable set of values as well as planning and management systems. The greenways are expanding because they are consensual and because they link a recreational use of nature to the management systems. It is not the case of superior law from outside directing that the area be preserved, but rather responding to local preferences for why the natural areas should be managed as landscapes. In areas like the New York Adirondacks or Massachusetts' Martha's Vineyard island, which have a comprehensive land use system, or the Pine Barrens in New Jersey, Adirondacks type systems continue to work fine, but states are not adopting new programmes like these. What is being adopted instead is the Greenway approach.

The Greenways system in North America shares a great deal with the construct of the Draft European Landscape Convention. Greenways recognise the role of people in the landscape, their cultural and natural heritage. To keep both culture and nature alive there has to be an active management system to avert degradation or loss of such values. It seems to me that, at the root, landscape is a social concept. What can we say is truly "wild"? Certainly not my own wild Adirondacks where we have jet planes flying over. We can no longer look up and see a wild sky but a multitude of jet plane contrails and, at night, satellites crossing with the stars. Acid rain falls on the lakes, killing the fish with the result that 300 lakes in the Adirondacks cannot reproduce fish; acid rain is killing the maple trees at the edge of these mountains, a unique tree species in North America from which we derive our maple sugar. We do not have a "wild" area any more. If we do not manage these systems carefully we will see them nibbled away. We can manage our resources of nature as cultural resources, whether for agricultural, historic, religious, recreational or habitat reasons, but, to be successful in doing so, it is essential to integrate the stewardship of these resources so that the false dichotomy of saying that one is more important than the other is eliminated once and for all.

Is it not remarkable that while Europe is doing this wonderful work on the Draft European Landscape Convention and the Pan-European Biological and Landscape Diversity Strategy, comparable undertakings are sprouting up in the grass roots of towns and villages and States throughout North America? The North American greenways are emerging totally independently, as very little is known about the European draft Landscape Convention in North America. It is also remarkable that the World Bank convened a workshop last month, in Washington D.C., on the synergies in natural and cultural heritage and that it reviewed its plans to integrate cultural landscape and heritage in all the World Bank analysis and development projects.

Both natural and cultural heritage are compromised by thoughtless development of new roads and transport, new housing projects, new quarries, new drainage and dam systems as well as urban sprawl. Both natural and cultural heritage attract tourists, provide for the human spirit to grow and be refreshed and define our sense of place and our sense of homeland. Today the Greenways movement in Canada and in the United States represents a precedent, the same type of precedent that occurred a century ago when the first national parks were established. We are extending this concept beyond the boundaries of a park, into our own homes, into our backyards, our neighbourhoods. We are recognising that we must integrate these systems and it is very interesting to note that law has been brought to the forefront to help define them. Our legal systems for managing landscape are becoming more refined and sophisticated through the integration of all of the various cultural and economic parameters. This appears to me as an internationally very valuable step toward building the sustainable society that Agenda 21 contemplates.

Commentator: *Ms. Grethel Aguilar, Vice Chair, IUCN Commission on Environmental Law*

Even though landscape has not received much attention from policy makers, it is definitely a topic present in the mind of all human beings. This is so especially because landscapes are determined by the action and interaction of natural and human factors.

I come from Central America, a part of the world where landscapes represent the relation of people with the environment and, above that, underline the importance of sustainable use of natural resources. At the present time the region is confronted with a huge increase in foreign investments that go from producing bananas, pineapples, coffee, and sugar to the development of the tourism industry which implies hotel constructions, water channels and all kinds of infrastructure. This situation, combined with the need to recognise and give the necessary importance to landscapes, has placed Central America in a very difficult position, the position that we are all aware of: the need to have an equilibrium between development and conservation. We need to define this equilibrium, and I believe that conservation of landscapes with a realistic approach will help us with this work. I come from a region that has to deal with poverty as one of its main problems and at the same time is confronted with a growing market for new investment. So what we need is to look to the future and give to landscape an economic value and use it for tourism and other industries without forgetting three important steps:

- To manage the process of evolution of the landscapes.

- To work towards developing land use plans and landscapes planning legislation.

- To recognise and protect outstanding landscapes.

It is also very important to reaffirm the relationship of landscapes with the World Heritage Convention,[22] particularly in the field of cultural landscapes. A good example of this is to be found in Guatemala, where cultural landscapes mix with lake-sides and mountains designed by agricultural methods and traditional land use of the indigenous people. In Mesoamerica 15 million people are indigenous and they have a very special relationship with the land, which they call *"tierra madre"* or mother earth. Landscapes are part of their tradition but this relation is getting weaker day by day due to the accelerating economic and social changes.

I would also like to mention that in some national constitutions, like the 1948 Constitution of Costa Rica, the legislators had already reaffirmed the obligation of the Government and the citizens to conserve the scenic beauty of the country.

The Draft European Landscape Convention is not only relevant to Europe but also to the international community at large, because we all need to learn about use and conservation of landscapes. Once the draft convention is adopted and implemented, it will be something to watch closely so as to learn from that experience. It can be used as an instrument to call the attention of other parts of the world to such an important matter.

European Landscapes Systems
Systèmes Européens de Protection du Paysage

Cyrille de Klemm, *membre, Commission du droit de l'environnement de l'UICN; Vice Président, Société française pour le droit de l'environnement*

Je dois vous parler des systèmes européens de protection du paysage. C'est un titre un peu vague, je ne sais pas très bien ce que c'est qu'un système, mais je vais essayer d'identifier deux groupes d'institutions qui vont servir à protéger le paysage en Europe.

Le premier, c'est la création de zones de paysages protégés. C'est de celui-là que je vous parlerai le plus, parce que c'est le plus développé. Et puis, depuis quelque temps se dessinent des mesures générales de protection, non du paysage, mais d'éléments du paysage. Ce sera le sujet de ma deuxième partie.

Introduction

Les paysages protégés en Europe existent parce que il n'y a pas, réellement, de zones à l'état naturel complet, permettant l'institution de zones protégées du genre parc national - catégorie 2 de l'UICN; c'est à dire de grands espaces à l'état proche de l'état naturel, essentiellement sur des terres publiques, et sans occupation humaine. Cela n'existe en Europe que dans le "Grand Nord" ou dans

---

[22]   *Cf supra at N. 3.*

le "Grand Est" et, quelques fois, encore en montagne. Ce genre d'instrument n'est pas adapté à la situation européenne. La présence humaine ne pouvant généralement pas être exclue, il fallait essayer de trouver autre chose, d'où le succès de la catégorie de paysages protégés qui s'est maintenant développée d'une manière intense en Europe. Ces paysages protégés appartiennent à la catégorie 5 de la classification de l'UICN des zones protégées; il s'agit de paysages résultant de l'interaction de l'homme et de la nature, qui ont une valeur esthétique, culturelle et écologique. C'est cette interaction là qu'il s'agit de protéger. Cela ce fait par l'intermédiaire d'une institution qui s'appelle le parc naturel ou par la création de paysages protégés. Il n'y a pas réellement de séparation marquée entre ces deux types d'institutions, il s'agit plus de noms que d'autres choses. Mais d'une manière générale, le parc naturel est pourvu d'institutions gestionnaires qui permettent de mettre en oeuvre une véritable politique de protection, tandis que le simple paysage protégé est un fragment de territoire qui a été délimité sur une carte, où il existe une certaine réglementation de protection du paysage, mais où il n'y a, en général, pas d'institution particulière pour le gérer.

Les parcs naturels

Le parc naturel existe depuis longtemps, depuis 1889 en Angleterre, où on n'a cependant jamais pu se mettre d'accord sur une terminologie, les parcs nationaux étant en fait des parcs naturels. En France, c'est en 1973 que le concept de parc naturel régional a été reconnu par la loi, et a été renforcé d'ailleurs tout dernièrement. En Europe du Sud, c'est beaucoup plus récent: en Espagne c'est une loi de 1989 sur la conservation des espaces naturels et de la faune et flore sauvages qui institue cette catégorie; en Italie, c'est une loi de 1991 – loi cadre sur les aires protégées et au Portugal c'est une loi de 1993. On a aussi dans d'autres pays d'Europe la même institution, mais je ne puis vous faire un exposé complet de la situation des parcs naturels en Europe, car cela prendrait trop longtemps.

J'exposerai par contre rapidement l'objet de ces parcs. Si on prend, par exemple, la loi cadre italienne sur les aires protégées de 1991, elle nous dit qu'il doit s'agir d'espaces constituant des systèmes homogènes choisis pour leurs valeurs naturelles, paysagères ou esthétiques et pour les traditions culturelles des populations locales. Au Portugal, le Décret-loi de 1993 nous dit que les parcs naturels sont des espaces contenant des paysages naturels ou semi-naturels ayant un intérêt national, et constituant des exemples d'intégration harmonieuse des activités humaines et de la nature. En Pologne, la loi sur la conservation de la nature de 1991 appelle cela des "parcs de paysages", protégés pour leur valeur naturelle, historique et culturelle, l'objet étant d'harmoniser la protection avec des activités économiques, agricoles et de loisirs. Comme vous voyez, toutes ces définitions se ressemblent. Je prendrai aussi la définition française: il s'agit de territoires à l'équilibre fragile, au patrimoine naturel et culturel riche. Il s'agit à la fois de protéger ce patrimoine, de contribuer au développement économique et social du territoire en question, et de promouvoir l'accueil, l'éducation et l'information du public. Je terminerai par la Hongrie, où une loi de 1996 les appelle "réserves de protection du paysage", et nous dit qu'il s'agit, encore une fois, d'espaces de grandes dimensions, riches en valeurs naturelles et paysagères, auxquels les interactions entre l'homme et la nature ont donné un caractère esthétique, culturel et naturel particulier, et dont la fonction principale est la conservation d'éléments du paysage et des valeurs naturelles. On remarquera que cette définition insiste beaucoup plus sur les valeurs naturelles que sur les valeurs culturelles.

De manière générale, ces parcs, qu'ont-ils en commun? Je suis obligé d'être bref: il y a d'abord une réglementation qui varie beaucoup; certains systèmes ne constituent que des cadres incitatifs; cela est vrai, par exemple, pour les parcs nationaux anglais et les parcs naturels régionaux français. Mais dans d'autres cas, par exemple en Espagne, en Italie, au Portugal, en Grèce, en Pologne tout peut être réglementé dans un parc naturel. En France, des progrès récents ont été accomplis pour renforcer le statut des parcs naturels régionaux. Il s'agit de contrats qui sont conclus entre les collectivités publiques, essentiellement les communes concernées. Cette charte n'a qu'une valeur d'orientation, elle n'est pas opposable aux tiers. Elle n'est donc pas applicable directement pour les particuliers. Mais les plans d'occupation des sols des communes des parcs naturels régionaux doivent être compatibles avec la charte: c'est maintenant la loi qui le dit et donc cela représente, tout de même, une mesure contraignante. Les parcs, du moins les plus contraignants comme ceux d'Espagne, d'Italie, du Portugal, sont divisés en zones. Par exemple dans la communauté autonome espagnole de Madrid il y a un parc qui s'appelle "Cuenca Alta del Manzanares" qui comprend des réserves naturelles intégrales, des réserves naturelles, des zones agro-pastorales où les activités traditionnelles sont autorisées et favorisées, des zones de transition où des activités sportives, de loisirs, culturelles sont autorisées à condition qu'elles soient compatibles avec la conservation du parc et puis, finalement des zones urbanisables avec des règles particulières concernant la construction. Donc le parc est une mosaïque de zones où les contraintes peuvent variées considérablement d'une zone à l'autre selon l'intérêt de chaque zone pour la conservation.

Les parcs sont soumis en général à une législation proche de la législation d'urbanisme qui est souvent autonome. Comme ce sont des espaces habités, il est nécessaire d'articuler la réglementation de ces parcs avec la législation d'urbanisme. En Angleterre nous avons, peut-être, le système le plus équilibré, puisque le parc national anglais est une autorité compétente en matière d'urbanisme avec pouvoir d'établir les plans, les documents d'urbanisme du parc et accorder les permis de construire. Cela est assez remarquable et exceptionnel car, en général, même là où les parcs sont forts, les questions d'urbanisme restent en dehors de la compétence des autorités du parc. Il y a cependant la règle de la compatibilité qui joue: en Espagne, en Italie, au Portugal la réglementation du parc va s'imposer au règlement d'urbanisme et, s'il y a incompatibilité, les documents d'urbanisme, tels les plans d'occupation des sols, devront être révisés en conséquence.

Évidemment ceci ne résout pas le problème des activités qui ne relèvent pas du droit de l'urbanisme, ce qui est le cas en général de la plupart des activités agricoles, forestières et des activités de loisirs, à moins qu'elles n'impliquent la création d'infrastructures. Mais bien entendu, les règlements applicables aux parcs permettent de réglementer ces activités dans les pays où les parcs sont forts, comme, encore une fois, en Espagne, en Italie, au Portugal où l'on peut réglementer tout ce que l'on veut selon les zones. Par exemple, si je reprends le parc espagnol dont je parlais toute à l'heure, celui de "La Cuenca Alta del Manzanares", dans les zones sensibles pourront être interdites les cultures fourragères, les prairies artificielles, le reboisement ou l'introduction d'espèces non-indigènes.

Ces parcs sont gérés; il y a donc des autorités gestionnaires. En général il s'agit d'un organe collégial, qui est une sorte de conseil d'administration, et un directeur. Dans certains pays, la gestion se fait directement par l'administration centrale qui nomme un directeur. Il peut y avoir un comité consultatif; c'est le cas, par exemple, au Portugal ou en Espagne dans les différentes régions. Mais dans d'autres pays on a été nettement plus loin et le parc constitue un établissement public, ayant la personnalité juridique, ce qui lui facilite énormément la vie. Cela lui permet, par exemple de signer des contrats, d'acquérir directement des terres, sans être obligé de passer par l'administration centrale, en encore d'accorder directement des subventions. Les conseils d'administration, cependant, sont en général composés de représentants de l'administration publique et des collectivités locales, avec une certaine représentation des intérêts économiques de la région, des scientifiques et des organisations de protection de la nature. La prééminence, souvent, des représentants des collectivités locales peut, évidemment, poser quelques problèmes parce que c'est, après tout, le conseil d'administration qui va prendre des décisions souvent majeures. Si les collectivités locales prédominent, le conseil d'administration risque fort d'être juge et partie. D'un autre côté, si les autorités locales ne sont pas suffisamment représentées, elles ne voudrons tout simplement pas faire partie d'un parc et l'obstruction risque d'être considérable. Entre les deux maux je ne sais pas lequel il faut choisir; il faut, comme toujours, trouver le juste équilibre.

Se pose aussi la question de la compétence juridique des gestionnaires; dans certains pays ils n'en ont pratiquement pas. Par exemple en France, dans le parc naturel régional, il n'y a pas grand chose qui puisse être fait en matière de réglementation; en Angleterre non plus. Mais dans certains pays, la compétence des gestionnaires est extrêmement étendue. A la limite, nous avons par exemple l'Italie, où c'est l'autorité du parc qui constate les infractions, qui assure la perception des amendes administratives, et qui fait toute une série de règlements. Ceci aussi pose des problèmes:

les administrations ont horreur de se faire déposséder de leurs compétences ou prérogatives en faveur d'une entité comme un parc. Dans des pays comme la Grèce, même si la loi permet maintenant de créer ce genre de parc, et il en a été créé un ou deux, il n'a pas été possible de déposséder les administrations de leurs compétences; ceci fait que le gestionnaire n'a pratiquement aucun pouvoir et que l'administration continue à faire, dans le parc, ce qu'elle veut.

Finalement, il y a partout des plans de gestion qui, dans la plupart des cas, sont des simples documents d'orientation sans valeur réglementaire. Cela peut se tempérer, comme par exemple en Belgique dans la région Wallonne, où les autorités publiques sont obligées de motiver leurs décisions en regard du plan de gestion du parc; leur pouvoir discrétionnaire est donc un petit peu limité. Et puis il y a des pays, encore une fois l'Espagne, l'Italie, le Portugal où les plans de gestion ont une valeur réglementaire: ils sont adoptés par décret, ils sont obligatoires et ils sont très détaillés, zone par zone. Voilà en gros l'instrument du parc naturel.

Les paysages protégés

Je passe rapidement sur le deuxième instrument qui est le paysage protégé parce que, en fait, c'est un parc naturel de deuxième zone; on le trouve en général dans les pays qui ont déjà le parc naturel. Par exemple, au Portugal les parcs naturels sont des espaces d'intérêt national et le paysage protégé recouvre des zones de paysages naturels et semi-naturels, C'est la même définition, mais dans ce cas ils sont d'intérêt régional ou local, et le classement a pour effet de permettre l'adoption de mesures au niveau régional ou local pour le maintien et la valorisation du paysage et de la diversité écologique de ces espaces.

En Angleterre nous avons des zones de beauté naturelle exceptionnelle, "areas of outstanding natural beauty", où l'on cherche à limiter les activités qui peuvent porter atteinte au paysage. Par exemple, lorsque les autorités locales font leurs plans d'occupation des sols elles doivent au préalable, obligatoirement, consulter la Countryside Commission. Elles n'ont cependant pas l'obligation de suivre son avis. Cela peut avoir une certaine efficacité, mais ce n'est pas une protection très poussée. Le cas de la Norvège est intéressant, parce qu'il permet de créer des paysages protégés dans des communes où il n'existe pas de plan d'occupation des sols, alors que lorsqu'il en existe un, il est impossible de créer un paysage protégé. De plus, si le plan d'occupation des sols est établi après la création du paysage protégé, ce dernier devient nul et sans effet. En d'autres termes, on part d'une idée optimiste, à savoir que la protection d'un paysage peut être assurée par un plan d'occupation des sols et que ce n'est qu'en l'absence d'un tel plan qu'il y aura la possibilité de créer une zone de paysage protégé.

J'en vient maintenant, rapidement, à ma deuxième partie, concernant la protection du paysage en général.

La protection du paysage en général

Tout d'abord cela s'est fait par l'intermédiaire de différentes institutions de protection de la nature et notamment par la protection de certains types d'habitat. Dans certains pays, certains types d'habitats sont protégés d'office. Il n'est donc pas possible de les modifier ou de les altérer sans autorisation. Au Danemark, ce système existe depuis longtemps et couvre une superficie non négligeable. Il y a aussi des règles particulières d'urbanisme qui sont applicables à certaines régions sensibles. En France, par exemple, nous avons la loi littorale et la loi montagne, qui assurent une préservation du paysage. En Italie, la loi Galasso a le même objet, et donne une protection d'office à certains types d'espaces sensibles comme la montagne au dessus d'une certaine altitude, les rivages de la mer, et les bords des cours d'eau. Dans les pays scandinaves, nous avons aussi une législation très stricte sur les constructions le long des rivages; au Danemark, on protège ainsi les dunes et aussi les murets de pierre ou de terre, qui sont des véritables éléments du paysage.

Depuis quelque temps, on voit certains autres instruments apparaître. Un concept qui me paraît intéressant se trouve dans la loi slovaque de 1994 sur la protection de la nature et du paysage, une loi qui établi le concept de niveau de protection. Le "niveau 1" couvre l'ensemble du territoire, c'est à dire qu'il y a un certain nombre de règles qui sont applicables partout. Ensuite nous avons le "niveau 2" qui est le paysage protégé, et puis on monte la hiérarchie pour arriver au "niveau 5" qui est celui de la réserve naturelle intégrale. Ce qui permet, en Slovaquie, de faire des mosaïques et d'avoir des parcs qui sont composés de différentes zones de ce genre. Dans le cadre du niveau 1, par exemple, il faut, sur l'ensemble du territoire slovaque, une autorisation pour toute une série d'activités comme, entre autres, le drainage des zones humides, les plantations d'arbres, l'affichage, les grandes manifestations sportives et le brûlage de l'herbe.

On peut aussi imaginer des textes qui protègent certains éléments particuliers du paysage. Ceci s'inscrit dans le concept de réseau, notamment le réseau écologique pan-européen qui est en train de se mettre en place dans la cadre de la stratégie évoquée par Liz Hopkins. Je ne donnerai que deux exemple: Une protection réglementaire et une protection par la méthode incitative.

Une protection réglementaire existe par exemple dans la cas de la Belgique, région flamande, où il existe un texte de 1991 qui soumet à autorisation la destruction de la végétation naturelle et des éléments linéaires du paysage dans toute une série de zones; et puis un décret tout récent, du 21 octobre 1997, qui habilite le gouvernement flamand à prendre toute une série de mesures utiles pour la protection des petits éléments du paysage, pouvant aller jusqu'à l'interdiction de certaines activités, ou l'obligation d'obtenir une autorisation, ou encore soumettre certaines activités à une obligation de notification. Ces petits éléments du paysage sont énumérés; il s'agit vraiment de petits éléments, tels les accotements routiers, des arbres, des bosquets, des sources, des talus, des chemins creux, des vergers, des mares, des cours d'eau ou des haies. Voilà donc un instrument réglementaire qui va permettre une réglementation qui autrement est encore presque partout impossible.

Le deuxième exemple est celui de la protection par la méthode incitative comme celle pratiquée en Suisse où la Loi fédérale sur la protection de la nature et du paysage nous dit que dans les régions d'exploitation agricole intensive les Cantons doivent veiller à une compensation écologique sous forme de bosquets champêtres, de haies, de rives boisées et tout autre type de végétation naturelle adaptée à la situation. Le financement se fait par l'intermédiaire des Cantons. Comme cela ne suffisait pas, une loi fédérale récente permet d'accorder des aides directes au propriétaire, aides qui peuvent aller jusqu'à 3.000 SFrs. par hectare pour certains types de biotope, comme par exemple les prairies fleuries. En contrepartie, les agriculteurs doivent s'abstenir d'utiliser des engrais et n'ont pas le droit d'exploiter leurs prairies autrement que par la fauche.

Ces deux exemples, la voie réglementaire et la voie contractuelle, pourraient évidemment se combiner.

Conclusion

Peut-on dire que nous avons des systèmes du protection du paysage en Europe? Probablement oui pour les parcs naturels, où nous sommes arrivés à une sorte de catégorie intermédiaire entre la "Catégorie II" et la "Catégorie V" de l'UICN. Nous ne sommes pas en "Catégorie II" parce que certaines activités sont permises même dans certains parcs nationaux, et nous ne sommes pas vraiment en "Catégorie V" parce que nous avons, tout de même, des mesures de protection qui peuvent être très fortes à l'intérieur de ces parcs.

Encore quelques mots sur l'importance de la participation du public et des collectivités locales. Ici encore, il faut d'une part asseoir la légitimité des parcs, et d'autre part éviter leur paralysie; encore une fois, il faut trouver le juste équilibre. Pour les activités traditionnelles, il est évident que la réglementation ne suffit pas et que des contrats, des subventions, des aides, des conseils, un suivi, sont indispensables. Pour tout ceci il est nécessaire d'avoir un gestionnaire en contact avec les réalités écologiques, économiques et sociales. Il faut aussi, bien sûr, du personnel et de l'argent, c'est là que le bât blesse le plus souvent.

En dehors des zones protégées, la situation est toute différente. Partant de la protection de types d'habitats, on est passé à celle d'éléments du paysage, qui en eux-même sont fongibles et individuellement peu important pour la conservation mais qui, collectivement, ont une importance énorme. Peut-être la Convention sur le paysage rendra-t-elle nécessaires ces mesures de protection des petits éléments du paysage, à condition que l'on trouve des instruments satisfaisants. Comme je le disais ce matin, il faudrait essayer tous ensemble de trouver ces instruments, et de définer comment les mettre en oeuvre sur l'ensemble du territoire, c'est à dire sur le territoire qui bénéficie du premier niveau de protection. Ainsi, nous pourrons graduellement établir ce réseau qui reliera entre elles les zones protégées, à travers un paysage qui sera lui même en partie préservé.

Landscape Law Within African Environmental Law

Charles Okidi, *Vice Chair, IUCN Commission on Environmental Law; Founding Dean of the School of Environmental Studies of Moi University in Kenya; currently Task Manager for the UNEP/UNDP/Dutch Government Joint Project in Environmental Law and Institutions*

As Maurice Kamto could not make it to this colloquium I was asked to take his place and, as I was trying to make up my mind, I could feel my ancestors warning me that they would not forgive me if I did not rise to the occasion to talk about environmental law in Africa.

Africa is certainly a very diverse continent, with some 11.5 million square miles, more than 50 States, all members of the United Nations, a bewildering array of biodiversity in terms of landscapes, flora, fauna and, of course, people. All these elements together constitute the landscapes of Africa. Obviously, taking on the task of making a presentation on law relating to landscapes, without advanced notice, in Paris, in the midst of other conferences and meetings is quite a challenge. This type of discussion has to be based on facts and on law, and if you have not already pieced them together it becomes extremely difficult to present this topic. I did, however, pluck up courage and I took refuge in an adage I learned from American litigation lawyers long ago: "When law is on your side, use law; when facts are on your side, use facts, and when neither of those are on your side, yell like hell". So I thought to myself: well I have three options but as I have not brought with me, from Africa, the facts and the law, I could try yelling like hell.

The African continent has a great diversity of geophysical forms: forests, vegetative cover, wildlife and the human beings that interact with them. Left to themselves, the vegetative cover and the geophysical forms would probably retain a pristine setting. But, in reality, this is not the case. There is considerable interference by human beings and, therefore, regulations and legal regimes for purposes of intervention to maintain a measure of equilibrium have been adopted. It is not likely that there are many laws in Africa addressing the question of landscapes as such. Provisions relating to landscape are found in the physical planning laws of the various countries and this suggests something quite specific: management of landscapes, regulations and legal regimes for management of landscapes are intertwined with human interaction. The question raised earlier on whether or not it is possible, feasible or even desirable to talk about landscapes without taking into account the interaction with human population, human settlement and, of course, the question of sustainable utilisation of natural resources, is a pertinent one. The laws relating to physical planning in the African setting largely relate to the utilisation of space and of natural resources by the human element in it.

With the limited information that I have I would simply like to give you a presentation in two parts. First I will present the general structure of the laws that exist in the African setting, using examples from three African countries: South Africa, Nigeria and Kenya. I will then mention some of the recent developments, the recent pressures on the very process of implementation of those legal regimes and the kind of chaotic situation catapulting a few of the African countries. I am being cautious by saying a few, but in the future, it is likely that some of that pressure will sweep through many countries in Africa. The examples I will use are intended to give you an idea of the types of laws that are emerging within the context of physical planning, as well as the institutional structures and processes used for the implementation of those laws.

The Legal Structure

Given the time and the resources it is hardly possible for me to give a detailed analysis of the general landscape of laws relating to landscapes in Africa. From Southern Africa I shall briefly mention the ensemble of laws that exist in the Republic of South Africa. I shall then move to the West with the physical planning law in Nigeria and finish with the case of Kenya.

For about ten years the Physical Planning Act (N. 88 of 1967) remained in force in South Africa in its original formulation, but within the last 30 years this law has undergone 11 major amendments, which are the following:

Physical Planning and Utilisation of Resources Amendment Act, N. 73 of 1975;
Environment Planning Amendment Act, 1977;
Environment Planning Amendment Act, 1981;
Physical Planning Amendment Act, 1983;
Physical Planning Amendment Act, 1984;
Then a similar Act adopted in 1985, followed by Regional Services Councils Act, 1985;
Transfer of Powers and Duties of the President, 1986 relating to the power of the President to control the use of land and resources;
Environment Conservation Act, 1989 which still largely remains the framework law of South Africa;
KwaZulu-Natal Joint Services Act, 1990;
Physical Planning Act, 1991.

Clearly, this array of amendments to the Physical Planning Act of 1967 largely modifies it, and practically repeals it, but it still remains in the Statute books with the residual provisions that are still in force.

Just to summarise and to give you the scope, let me read from the Statute which states its purpose as follows:

- "To promote coordinated environment planning and the utilisation of the Republic's resources for those purposes;

- to provide for control of the zoning and subdivision of land for industrial purposes;

- for reservation of land for industrial purposes;

- for the establishment of such controlled areas;

- for restriction of subdivision and use of land in controlled areas;

- for purposes of compilation and approval of guide plans;

- for restrictions upon the use of land for certain purposes."

Physical planning law describes largely the main features of what it controls and the processes used. I have not been able to get exact information on the process of getting physical planning adopted for specific areas. That would be very interesting from the point of view of public participation in view of the laws that were adopted during the Apartheid era.

In Western Africa, The Nigerian Urban and Regional Planning Decree, 1992, Decree N.88, provides for the different competencies. Nigeria has a federal system and, therefore, there is federal, state and urban physical planning which also includes land use. At the local level, or in the urban setting, the governing and controlling institution is the Authority which initiates and develops local physical and development plans and receives petitions.

One of the requirements at all three levels – local or urban, state and federal – is that the physical planning act adopted at each level must be gazetted and publicised in at least two, widely read, national newspapers. Whether two newspapers is a sufficient way of exposing a planned decree to the population is highly questionable, but at least it is an attempt to reach out to the population to get inputs, especially from professional bodies, on whether they agree with the physical development plans. Various stakeholders submit their petitions, which are taken into account for the revisions, then the local development plan moves to the state level, where a board coordinates and harmonises the various physical development plans applying to both rural and urban areas. It also receives petitions, objections and requests for corrections. All this is collated and moved on to the federal level where the Federal Commission has the responsibility, not only for the development of the physical development plan for the country as a whole, but also for enunciating the federal policies and the federal regulations. So the movement is both upwards and downwards in terms of getting the instructions from the federal level in order to provide for formulation of the national policies and develop the national physical development plan. Petitions are received and taken into account at the federal level, before the physical development plan is submitted to the respective ministers for the issue of the decrees. Probably, as we will see in the case of Kenya, my third example, the powers of the Boards, the powers of the Commissions under the Authorities seem to fall immediately under the Ministers, without any other check off process, except perhaps in the case of Nigeria with the application of environmental impact assessments as the only other intervening mechanism through which the planned national physical development machinery can be circumvented. But, essentially, the powers of the executive seem to be overwhelming in the Nigerian system. The national physical development plans in Nigeria remain in operation for five years, after which they are subject to review, going through the same process again. As I have mentioned, Nigeria has a National Environmental Impact Assessment Decree. It is quite comprehensive, largely drawing its inspiration from the USA Environmental Protection Agency and its EIA procedures. However, the question of enforcement at national level still remains.

In Kenya, the Physical Planning Act was adopted in 1996; it deals with physical planning in both urban and rural areas. It replaced both the old Land Planning Act, which formerly applied to rural areas and to land in urban areas, and the Town Planning Act, which used to apply to urban centres. Kenya's environmental legislation does not provide for an environmental impact assessment, as is the case in Nigeria, but largely, except for the fact that Nigeria has a federal system, the structure of the law is quite similar. Kenya's legislation provides for development of a national physical development plan, the commission in charge of its implementation can receive petitions, objections and do amendments before the final physical planning act is adopted.

Also in 1996, Kenya adopted the Physical Planners Registration Act, which determines the competencies in terms of professional abilities. There is a registration process for national physical planners, and the required qualifications for all intervenants are specified.

This is the legislation in place; it puts into place procedures for physical planning in both rural and urban areas, but what exactly happens in practice is quite a different story.

The Practice

First of all I will briefly mention some of the compelling pressures on this machinery, which is tidy and allows for a reasonable level of governance in terms of physical planning in order to ensure the protection of critical landscapes or those to be set aside for specific purposes.

The first pressure, which is a legitimate one, arises from the international commodities market. Kenya, like most other African countries, is basically an agricultural country. What happens is that the secular decline in the returns from agricultural commodities in the international market compels countries to produce more and more with the perverse result that increased production increases the offer, which in turns lowers the prices of the commodities and reduces the returns. It was this economic finding, in the late 50s early 60s, that led to the creation of UNCTAD in 1964: the realisation that developing countries were suffering because of declining returns from the commodities they produce to sell on the international market. This increasing pressure to use more and more land for agricultural purposes, particularly for cash crops like coffee, tea or pyrethrum, is affecting the most fertile lands in the country. Some of the most delectable landscapes suffer from this opening to agriculture. This is a difficult pressure to resist and I believe that more environmentalists should participate in the negotiations for commodities agreements, alongside developing countries' representatives, to give restraining advice.

The second element of pressure is the increase in population. As we have seen in the case of Asia, Africa also has one of the highest trends of population increase. This pressure affects the human/wildlife interfaces, the human/forestry interfaces and the forestry/wildlife interfaces. The conflictual situations arise from human/wildlife interfaces as well as human/forestry interfaces. The conflicts arising in human/wildlife interfaces manifest themselves in poaching of wildlife. The legal regime imprisons people for poaching, yet the people, used to living in the traditional way, do not understand why they should go to jail for practising what their ancestors have transmitted to them; animals were hunted for food and for ceremonies. It is hard to accept and respect a law that is so distant from traditional beliefs. This means that the legal regime has to be adjusted, so that instead of putting people into prisons, those concerned with the management of wildlife can reach the local population to explain the need for conservation of wildlife and make them partners in the management of wildlife rather than poachers. In practice, convicting someone to a jail sentence does not solve the problem. When the individual returns, not even understanding why he spent time in jail, the wildlife in his neighbourhood will not be safe.

This type of situation makes it clear that what is required is a change of modalities. The issue is not that because people are poor they should be allowed to kill wildlife; the job can only be done through education and increased awareness of the local population. There is a need to work in partnership with the local people and explain to them why the changes are necessary. We need to adopt laws that provide for management regimes, that provide alternatives for the people, for their livelihood. The same kind of argument applies to forestry reserves where local people cut trees for personal needs. It is important to get the local people involved in the management system itself, to diversify their sources of income and let them understand that there are alternatives for their livelihood. This is a very sensitive topic because it is tied to the tariffs of energy, like electricity for instance. Every time electricity tariffs increase, people will try to reduce the impact on their budget by using charcoal and wood for fuel. What is to be done? The governments must provide the local population with new, renewable and affordable energy resources, rather than relying on imported hydrocarbon. There is a need for reorientation of the legal regime to include more of the management imperatives and incentives to move away from reliance on the elements that destroy the landscapes.

Another perverse development is generally associated with the Bretton Woods community. It is the trend towards privatisation. As governments must not own any land, government officials immediately move to allocate whatever may be called government land, that could be preserved as public land for purposes of preservation of landscapes, to individuals for purposes of development. This does not benefit the poor people; we can't say here, as is often heard, that the poor people are responsible for the destruction of the environment. Invariably, those who benefit from government allocations in terms of privatisation are the wealthiest of the society, who also wield the political clout. This trend has increased gradually. In Kenya, the terminology used to define this trend is "grabiosis" or the ailment that compels people to grab property whenever possible. It is a critical situation, which has catapulted the country into a near crisis at times, because often there is encroachment on forest lands. This tendency to acquire land provokes the removal of reserved lands from the gazette to be allocated to private individuals who exploit them for cultivation but also for development of housing schemes.

On 7 October of this year, the environmental groups in Kenya discovered that the middle of one of the largest indigenous forest lands, adjoining Nairobi, Karura forest, had been allocated to private individuals and was already being dug up by machinery for purposes of road construction and drainage systems. A feeling which can be described as a mixture between fury, anger and desperation compelled environmental groups, with 12 members of Parliament in the lead, to invade the site. The workers fled in every direction and everything, including buildings and heavy engines used on the construction site, was burned down. Over 80 million Kenyan Shillings (about 2 million $US) worth of property was lost. This kind of extreme behaviour, even though understandable as a reaction to an extreme situation of destruction of landscape and natural vegetation, is hardly sustainable. There must be better, more legitimate ways to solve these issues rapidly and effectively. The members of Parliament who were present on the site could have used the legal means at their disposal, like amending the legislation and ensuring more effective enforcement. But I would like to stress that there is also a need to strengthen the judiciary, to provide for effective recourse in this type of situation. Environmental jurisprudence is still at the formative stage. There is a need to strengthen the judiciary through capacity building initiatives and to spread the information about recent case law from different jurisdictions, so that law suits for environmental issues can be seen as a viable option by the people concerned. Unfortunately, in many countries in Africa, the judiciary seems to be either incompetent, or politically correct, or corrupt. Therefore, like in the above example, people tend to choose manifestations of anger and destruction rather than hoping for their case to be solved by the judiciary. There is also a very urgent need to sharpen the professional competence of people in the NGO movements. In the late 80s, early 90s, the western donor countries said "Governments in many developing countries are corrupt, therefore we will go to NGOs". But they didn't realise that the NGOs occupants are also products of the same system described as corrupt. There was a major move towards the NGO field without much assessment of their professional competence. It is desirable to strengthen the competence of the people working in the NGO movements in the environmental field. The same argument goes for lawyers at the bar. Like the judges, they should be made aware of some of the emerging case law. In India, the Supreme Court case M.C.Mehta v. Kamal Nath and others[23] succeeded on the basis of the public trust doctrine. Can this be tried in other jurisdictions? In the Philippines, the Oposa case[24] succeeded on the basis of intergenerational equity, relying, of course, also on the 1987 Constitution of the Philippines; but the Court took clear judicial notice of the significance of intergenerational equity. I would like to emphasise that, in order to allow for the development of protection of landscapes in Africa, involving public participation, there is a need for stronger legislation but also a need for a stronger judiciary.

Commentator: *Lyle Glowka, Legal Officer, IUCN Environmental Law Centre*

I would like to say that it is a great honour and pleasure for me to be here and sit on this very distinguished panel of experts, a multicultural panel, to present my views. What I would like to do is not to comment directly on Charles Okidi's and Cyrille de Klemm's presentations but, rather, in the context of my area of specialisation, biodiversity, indirectly comment on what he and the other speakers have said thus far this afternoon.

I am rather new to the landscape conservation area; as I have said I work on biological diversity issues so I tend to look at things through biological diversity glasses. But it is the diversity of

---

[23]   Writ Petition No.182 of 1996, decided on December 13, 1996.

[24]   *Minors Oposa* v. *Secretary of the Department of the Environment and Natural Resources*, Decision of the Supreme Court of the Philippines, 30 July 1993, ILM vol. 33/1, pp. 174-206.

landscapes and seascapes, interacting with climatic variations and with a third variable, human intervention, in particular human use of biological resources, which, in fact, gives rise to biological diversity. This applies in Europe and all around the world.

If you are not familiar with the concept of biological diversity, please allow me to explain it. It tends to be associated with strict nature conservation, but it is actually a broader concept. When we talk about biological diversity we are talking about three ways of describing life on Earth: ecosystem diversity, species diversity and genetic diversity. The emphasis, therefore, is on life's variety at three different levels. So, really, what we are talking about is an attribute of life whose tangible manifestations – ecosystems, populations or species and genomes – give rise to the diversity of life that we have on earth.

To conserve biological diversity, or the variety of life on earth, we have to focus our actions on the tangible manifestations – the components of biological diversity – in order to maintain that variety. Land and seascape conservation is one tool that we can use to encourage and support biological diversity conservation.

One of the things that I have been struck by, since this conference started this morning, is the many terms and approaches that seem to be common to the areas of biodiversity conservation and the land and seascape conservation. What has struck me the most is that the erosion of land and seascapes is a very insidious process just as biological diversity loss is. We do not really recognise that it is happening until it is gone. Then it is too late. The loss of land or seascape is just as irretrievable as the loss of biodiversity. I think that this is a very important point to make because that means that, perhaps, our approaches to addressing both problems may be similar.

The insidiousness of both problems may also mean that we have to evolve ways that better address the creeping nature of landscape and biodiversity loss. As Charles Okidi said, we may need to adopt not only prescriptive approaches, but also enabling approaches: in other words, legal systems which would encourage people to conserve biological diversity at all three levels, perhaps through conservation of landscapes and seascapes.

This means that we are going to have to educate decision-makers and policy-makers to expand their view to the ecosystem level, the level at which a mosaic of land and seascapes (and biodiversity) is found. The legal systems we should strive for ought to encourage people to take an ecosystem approach, and encourage uses that support the conservation and sustainable use of constituent land and seascapes, and within these, their biological and non-biological components. Management systems and their underlying legal and institutional frameworks have not traditionally done this. Not only do we have to do this, but we also have to address some of the perversities that drive economic behaviour and the consequent erosion of landscapes and biological diversity in the first place.

Charles Okidi has commented on some of the underlying causes of landscape erosion and biological diversity loss in Africa. These are very systemic: commodity prices, demographic shifts and also, shifts towards privatisation. I agree with him, these are the real causes underlying both areas. There are others as well, many of which are country-specific. We need to identify these underlying causes in the national biodiversity planning processes established by the Convention on Biological Diversity, evaluate their legal and economic bases, and develop and apply combinations of legally-based prescriptive and incentive measures adapted to the particular threats in a country. We need to do all of these things if we are ever going to begin to overcome the erosion of land and seascapes and ultimately support biological diversity conservation.

CONCLUSIONS

Reflections on the Significance of the Themes Discussed at the Colloquium

Adrian Phillips, Chair, IUCN World Commission on Protected Areas; former Director General of the Countryside Commission of England and Wales; Professor, Cardiff University, UK

Thank you very much, it has been a privilege to be here. I have learned something about lawyers, which is that you really do believe in the power of words and have very little time for visual aids. I think I now understand why the projector went wrong. It was the collective feeling amongst all of you that this was an inappropriate way to communicate. Anyhow, I shall use no visual aids at this stage. I wanted to offer you a general thought on today's event, then outline three challenges before us, stemming from the general thought, and finally suggest three possible areas of work.

The general thought is that landscape is emerging as the new frontier for environmental law. This may be an ambitious statement as the concept of landscape is an ancient and universal one. In this connection, I like the phrase *tierra madre* which described it at one stage, but its incorporation into environmental law has been so far very limited. It has been quite clear from today's contributions that it is often addressed through other forms of legislation. It certainly has not received the level of attention that, for example, biodiversity, conservation or pollution control have received. But I think things may be changing. Landscape, as we have heard today, is an important concept because:

- it is inclusive;

- it brings together different interests in the cultural and natural environment;

- it is integrative, not only does it bring the cultural and natural environment together, but it looks at the relationship between them;

- it is participatory, with very strong emphasis on people involvement; and

- it is universal; landscape occurs everywhere, in town and country, in areas that have been very little touched by humans, as well as in areas that have undergone much modification.

Therefore, I believe that "landscape" is, indeed, a very appropriate focus for addressing many of the sustainable development/Agenda 21 issues.

The proposition I have put to you, that landscape is now emerging as the new frontier for environmental law, carries with it a number of important challenges.

The first challenge, I believe, is to develop legal approaches which link the previously separate concerns for environmental protection and for heritage protection and land use. In most countries we have separate laws for pollution control, biodiversity protection, conservation of the built heritage, architectural heritage and so forth. We have seen with the story of the World Heritage Convention,[25] how difficult it is to bring together the natural and the cultural, and yet it is in that nexus of the two that the real power of the concept of landscape lies. So I think that the first challenge for us, lawyers and environmental managers, is to see how those formerly separate elements can come together.

---

[25]   *Cf supra at N. 3.*

The second challenge is to extend the legal framework beyond the concern with protection to include landscape management, planning and creation. Lawyers, and, indeed, I think environmentalists generally, are very good at regulating, stopping people doing things, it comes naturally to us. But the point about landscape is that we have to put an equal, if not greater emphasis, upon encouraging what is positive in the care of the environment, taking a proactive role. What is the role of law in facilitating this, what is the role of law in encouraging the advice and incentive structures that bring that about? These are questions that will need to be considered.

The third challenge is to identify what is the appropriate level for dealing with landscape issues. And in particular what is proper to do at the international level, as opposed to the essentially local and national level at which these topics have been addressed in the past. Why should we undertake work at the international level? In the presentation on the European Convention, I suggested why it might be appropriate for Europe, but I think we need to be very clear on what is the added value from addressing this topic at the international level.

Finally, I would like to mention three areas for work which perhaps come out of that analysis. First, I think there is a need for comparative work on what is being done at the national level for addressing the landscape agenda. What are different countries doing in this area? Some have special landscape legislation, but others use general legislation related to land use, to protected areas and to historic buildings for this purpose. A particular area of work, in which the two IUCN Commissions might collaborate, is looking at the legal basis for Category V Protected Areas, the kind of work that Cyrille de Klemm mentioned, particularly its relevance and application in other parts of the world, outside Europe. Also, the Commissions could collaborate on some of the work that was suggested on an annex to the Convention, in compiling information on the different approaches to landscape protection, planning and management.

The second potential area for co-operation could be an examination of the capacity of international instruments to promote landscape protection, management and planning. We know, and welcome, the specific function in relation to the World Heritage Convention, but what is the role, if any, of the Convention on Biological Diversity? We just heard some suggestions from Lyle Glowka about that. What is the connection with the Ramsar Convention and so forth. How far are other international instruments fitted or capable of being used to promote the landscape agenda?

A final area of co-operative work could be the development of regional initiatives in other parts of the world, outside Europe. I am not suggesting that every region in the world needs to have a landscape convention, but I think that work on capacity development through training workshops under the auspices of IUCN's Environmental Law Commission, possibly jointly with other IUCN Commissions, could be a very appropriate programme of work. There are other parts of the world that, I suspect, would be quite excited about taking this item into the programme.

One participant left us with this lovely idea of "dream no small dreams". That ought to be the message we take away from here.

Nicholas A. Robinson, *Chair, IUCN Commission on Environmental Law; Professor, School of Law, Pace University*

I am struck by the common themes that ran through the day and, in concluding, I can only briefly note them.

There is a real need for linking the legal framework and technical planning to better manage landscape. This colloquium has discussed in some detail the importance of the better protection, management and planning of European landscapes this morning. That was the inspiration for our panel. And in this connection, I heard that there was strong support for a call for a closer working relationship between the technical and policy work in the PBLDS Action Theme 4, and the development of the Draft European Landscape Convention. From the comments heard, both in the colloquium and in informal conversations, it appears that there is a strong feeling that the above initiatives should join forces. It struck me that the same dialogue needs to exist within IUCN. For instance, our natural resources planners in IUCN are engaged in an exercise called the sustainable use initiative, to look at ways to ensure that any use of natural resources is sustainable. And yet, those dialogues are entirely divorced from anything we have heard here today, in terms of the development of legislation in Europe and other regions. We need to bring this development of landscape law together with the sustainable use initiative, to get the technical experts to talk to the legal experts.

It seems to me that landscapes are of such fundamental importance that our traditional work on protected landscapes needs to be recalled. Cyrille de Klemm has already done that very ably, but I would like to report to you the good news I recently had from the President of IUCN, Yolanda Kakabadse. The joint efforts of the World Commission on Protected Areas (WCPA) and the Commission on Environmental Law (CEL) on management of protected areas have produced a Draft Code of Conduct for Transboundary Protected Areas in Times of Peace and Armed Conflict. Yolanda Kakabadse, in her capacity as Minister of the Environment of Ecuador, was able to use this draft in the peace negotiations with Peru, to settle the boundary dispute between the two countries. A peace agreement was announced earlier this week. Here is an example where the use of protected areas gave a landscape value to peace: both countries have established a park on their side of the contested border. The area has 300 landmines, so it is not very safe yet, but rather than continue to fight over how to divide the resources, they are creating a protected area landscape which people will eventually be able to enjoy and understand as a nature park.

Therefore, while we talk about new frontiers of landscapes, we must not forget that the traditional protected areas still have a very important function. The protected area system is still a rather fragile system, in many parts of the world, and we need to nurture it and build it. In this regard, what we have heard today, about new developments of law, is very important, but it should not be at the expense of reaffirming the juridical foundation for much of what we do. At this point I would like to mention the UNESCO World Heritage Convention;[26] we need to expand and strengthen its operations and strengthen the integration of cultural and natural heritage under this convention.

Having said this, I take up your challenge Cyrille, I think your comments were brilliant and insightful; I think we need to develop a working group in the Law Commission to take a look at the legal basis for the Category V Protected Areas, as Adrian has also suggested. But we also need to use our unique legal background and experience to take a look at the legal instruments, the tools that are in the appendix to the Draft European Landscape Convention and elaborate these, not just so that when the Landscape Convention becomes operative in Europe there will be greater thinking and discussion, but also so that the same tools can be used all around the world. If there is one theme that came out of all of the comparative law analysis we heard today, it is that we are all struggling with the same phenomena, trying to help people preserve and manage their landscapes for a better quality of life. So I thank you for that suggestion, I shall take it to the Steering Committee of the Law Commission for action and invite other commissions to cooperate.

Jérôme Fromageau, *Président, Section Île de France, Société française pour le droit de l'environnement; Vice-doyen, Faculté Jean Monnet, Université de Paris Sud; membre Commission du droit de l'environnement de l'UICN*

Je voudrais simplement revenir brièvement sur deux thèmes qui ont été abordés à plusieurs reprises au cours de cette journée. En premier lieu, il me semble que le concept de paysage fait référence

---

[26] World Heritage Convention, Paris, 16 November 1972, 1037 UNTS 151.

au sensible, à la constitution de la mémoire. Historiquement, c'est un fait et s'il y a problème aujourd'hui à propos du paysage, c'est sans doute, comme on vient de le voir, parce que dans la plupart de nos sociétés, qu'elles soient européennes, africaines, américaines, asiatiques, il y a perte d'identité. Il est clair qu'il y a une très forte interaction nature/culture, une symbolique constructive très forte dans les paysages de qualité. Dans les sociétés traditionnelles le paysage est riche, et sur le plan de cette symbolique constructive et sur le plan de la biodiversité, il y a une participation minutieuse des populations locales à la gestion de l'espace.

C'est peut-être ce que nous ne savons plus faire, mais il est tout à fait extraordinaire de constater à quel point certaines expériences qui sont menées, à l'heure actuelle, pour réhabiliter, par exemple, des zones humides, reprennent, plus au moins implicitement, des anciens usages, des anciennes coutumes qui permettaient précisément à ces paysages de se construire et de se maintenir. Je crois qu'il faut systématiquement avoir ce problème à l'esprit. J'évoquais la référence au sensible, la constitution de la mémoire, il me semble qu'au fond, on a cherché à protéger la nature et donc aussi à protéger le paysage, à partir du moment, précisément, où l'homme n'avait plus de repère identitaire.

En second lieu, il convient de ne pas négliger les aspects urbains et périurbains du paysage, Je sais bien que ce n'est pas vraiment la vocation de l'UICN mais cela me paraît tout de même important. D'ailleurs, au travers d'un certain nombre d'interventions, en particulier celle du Doyen Charles Okidi, on a bien vu à quel point la question démographique, la question des infrastructures, la question de l'urbanisme en général est tout à fait fondamentale. Pourquoi faudrait-il continuer à accepter, de manière inexorable, comme si nous étions voués au fatalisme, que nos cités, nos grandes conurbations soient trop souvent inesthétiques, sales et polluées?

Au delà de ces réflexions, je voudrais, encore une fois, remercier tous le intervenants d'être venus ici à Paris. Sachez que notre groupe de juristes de la Société française pour le droit de l'environnement, est extrêmement sensible au fait que vous ayez choisi notre association et Paris pour marquer le 50e anniversaire de l'Union mondiale pour la nature.

Concluding Remarks

Cyrille de Klemm, *au nom de Gilles Martin, Président, Société française pour le droit de l'environnement*

C'est la troisième fois que je prends la parole devant vous aujourd'hui, mais ce n'est pas de ma faute, et je ne vous ennuierai pas avec une synthèse supplémentaire. Celles qui ont été faites par Adrian Phillips, Nick Robinson et Jérôme Fromageau suffisent largement. On m'a demandé, en effet, de prononcer ces quelques mots de clôture parce que le président de la Société française pour le droit de l'environnement, Gilles Martin, n'a malheureusement pas pu se joindre à nous aujourd'hui, étant donné ses très nombreuses tâches. C'est donc en ma qualité de vice-président de cette société que je prends la parole pour clôturer ces débats.

La Commission du droit de l'environnement fête ici, à sa manière, le 50ème anniversaire de l'UICN. Loin des fastes de Fontainebleau, elle a préféré se réunir à Paris, un peu à l'avance, plus calmement, parce que, bien entendu un certain nombre de personnalités assisteront après au fastes de Fontainebleau. Le Comité directeur de la Commission s'est réuni et à décidé de tenir ce colloque. Ce colloque est, à mon avis, un événement tout à fait fantastique, extraordinaire, car depuis qu'existe la Commission, ou du moins depuis que j'en suis membre, environs 30 ans, il n'y a jamais eu de colloque comme celui-ci. Non seulement ce colloque se tient avec les membres de la Commission et ses invités : on a fait appel aux juristes de l'environnement, aux membres de la Société française pour le droit de l'environnement et à tous ceux que cela pouvait intéresser. Non seulement sommes nous entre nous, nous avons aussi bénéficié de la collaboration entière et totale de la Commission des aires protégées de l'UICN, représentée par son Président, Adrian Phillips.

Ceci est tout à fait exceptionnel, permettez-moi de vous le dire. De plus, le Président de la Commission de survie des espèces, David Brackett, s'est joint à nous ce soir, et donc nous avons trois présidents de commissions de l'UICN dans cette salle. Je crois que c'est un précédent extrêmement important, extrêmement utile. Il faut donc essayer de continuer sur cette voie, c'est à dire organiser des colloques semblables dans l'avenir et accroître la coopération entre nos commissions. Ayant dit cela, je voudrais simplement remercier d'abord ceux qui ont eut l'idée de ce colloque et là je crois que Nick Robinson, Adrian Phillips et Françoise Burhenne-Guilmin ont partagé cette responsabilité. Merci donc à tous les trois, c'est très important que nous soyons ici ensemble ce soir. Mais si ce colloque a été un succès, c'est aussi à beaucoup d'autres que nous le devons et je renouvelle les remerciements qui ont déjà été exprimés ce matin envers le Sénat français et la Fondation Gaz de France. Et puis, en tant que représentant de la Société française pour le droit de l'environnement, qui je vous le rappelle, est membre de l'UICN, je voudrais remercier la Société française pour le droit de l'environnement Île de France, son Président, Jérôme Fromageau, et sa secrétaire générale Isabelle Trinquelle, qui n'ont pas ménagé leurs efforts pour assurer ce succès. Je voudrais aussi remercier mes collègues interprètes, Claudine Pierson-Viscovi et Charles Speed, mes collègues car, comme vous le savez, j'ai fait ce métier très longtemps et je le fait encore à l'occasion. Je remercie aussi les étudiants du DESS de diplomatie de l'Université de Paris Sud que Jérôme a su mobiliser pour cette réunion; ils ont fort bien assuré l'accueil. Finalement, je voudrais remercier les participants, parce que, sans les participants, il n'y aurais pas de colloque et ils sont venus très nombreux. Merci beaucoup.

Parvez Hassan, *Chairman*

I would also like to thank all the speakers and the commentators on this panel, for the brilliant insights and their hard work which has contributed to the success of this colloquium. I would personally like to thank the two IUCN Commission Chairs, Adrian Phillips and Nick Robinson, for the excellent co-sponsorship of this colloquium. A better way to celebrate the 50th anniversary of IUCN I could not have imagined. And to all this energy came the generous support of the French Society for Environmental Law and Jérôme Fromageau. I also want to thank the participants who added to the success of the colloquium.

ANNEX 1 A

Draft European Landscape Convention

Congress of Local and Regional Authorities of Europe, 5th session, Strasbourg, 26-28 May 1998, Council of Europe, Recommendation 40 (1998)

Projet de Convention européenne du paysage

Congrès des pouvoirs locaux et régionaux de l'Europe, 5me session, Strasbourg, 26-28 Mai 1998, Conseil de l'Europe, Recommandation 40 (1998)

PREAMBLE	PREAMBULE
The signatory states hereto,	Les Etats signataires de la présente Convention,
1. Considering that the aim of the Council of Europe is to achieve a greater unity between its members for the purpose of safeguarding and realising the ideals and principles which are their common heritage and that this aim is pursued in particular through agreements in the economic and social fields;	1. Considérant que le but du Conseil de l'Europe est de réaliser une union plus étroite entre ses membres, afin de sauvegarder et promouvoir les idéaux et les principes qui sont leur patrimoine commun et que ce but est poursuivi en particulier par la conclusion d'accords dans les domaines économique et social;
2. Concerned to achieve sustainable development based on a balanced and harmonious relationship between individuals, society and economic activity and the environment;	2. Soucieux de parvenir à un développement durable fondé sur un équilibre harmonieux entre l'individu, la société, l'économie et l'environnement;
3. Noting that landscape, as a complex element of the environment, has an important public-interest role in the cultural, ecological and social fields and constitutes an economic resource which, if properly managed, can contribute to job creation;	3. Notant que le paysage, en tant qu'élément complexe de l'environnement, de l'aménagement du territoire et de l'urbanisme, assume d'importantes fonctions d'intérêt général, sur les plans culturel, écologique et social et constitue une ressource économique dont une gestion appropriée peut contribuer à la création d'emplois;
4. Aware that landscape is an essential feature of human surroundings, that it contributes to the formation of local cultures and that it is a basic component of the European natural and cultural heritage, contributing to human well-being and consolidation of the European identity;	4. Conscients que le paysage constitue un aspect essentiel du cadre de vie des populations, qu'il concourt à l'élaboration des cultures locales et qu'il représente une composante fondamentale du patrimoine culturel et naturel de l'Europe, contribuant à l'épanouissement des êtres humains et à la consolidation de l'identité européenne;
5. Observing that developments in agriculture, forestry, industrial and mineral production techniques and in town-planning, transport, infrastructure, tourism and recreation practices and, at a more general level, changes in the world economy have the effect of speeding up the transformation of landscapes;	5. Remarquant que les évolutions des techniques de production agricole, sylvicole, industrielle et minière et des pratiques en matière d'urbanisme, de transport, de réseaux, de tourisme et de loisirs et, plus généralement, les changements économiques mondiaux ont pour effet d'accélérer la modification des paysages;
6. Wishing to satisfy the desire of populations to play an active part in the development of landscapes and to enjoy high-quality landscapes;	6. Désirant satisfaire le souhait des populations de jouer un rôle actif dans l'évolution des paysages et de jouir d'un paysage de qualité;
7. Believing that landscape, as a key element of individual and social well-being, entails rights and duties for everyone;	7. Persuadés que le paysage, élément essentiel du bien-être individuel et social, implique des droits et des devoirs pour chacun;
8. Having regard to the legal texts existing at international level in the field of protection and management of the natural and cultural heritage, regional/spatial planning, local self-government and transfrontier co-operation;	8. Ayant à l'esprit les textes juridiques existant au niveau international dans les domaines de la protection et de la gestion du patrimoine naturel et culturel, de l'aménagement du territoire, de l'autonomie locale et de la coopération transfrontalière;
9. Noting that no international legal instrument is devoted directly and comprehensively to the protection, management and planning of European landscapes;	9. Constatant qu'aucun instrument juridique international n'est consacré directement et globalement à la protection, à la gestion et à l'aménagement des paysages européens;

Have agreed as follows:

CHAPTER I - GENERAL PROVISIONS

Article 1: Definitions

For the purposes of the convention:

a. "Landscape" means a piece of territory, which may include coastal and/or inland waters, as perceived by populations, the appearance of which is determined by the action and interaction of natural and human factors;

b. "Landscape protection" means action to preserve a landscape's existing features, justified by its outstanding value derived from its special natural configuration or from the type of human activity for which it is used;

c. "Landscape management" means action to ensure the regular upkeep of a landscape and to harmonise changes which are necessary for economic and social reasons, from the point of view of sustainable development;

d. "Landscape planning" means action based on regional/spatial planning projects that are particularly forward-looking, with the aim of creating new landscapes according to the aspirations of the populations concerned;

e. "Landscape quality objective" means an expression by the competent public authorities of the aspirations of populations with regard to the landscape features of their surroundings.

Article 2: Scope

This convention applies to the entire European territory of the Parties and covers natural, rural, urban and peri-urban areas. It concerns ordinary or everyday landscapes no less than outstanding ones, since they all decisively influence the quality of the surroundings in which Europe's populations live.

Article 3: Aims

By this convention, each Party undertakes to ensure landscape protection, management and planning through the introduction of national measures and the organisation of European co-operation.

CHAPTER II - NATIONAL MEASURES

Article 4: Division of responsibilities

In its domestic legal system, each Party shall determine the best territorial level for implementing this convention according to its own division of responsibilities and in conformity with the principle of subsidiarity as defined by the European Charter of Local Self-Government.

Sont convenus de ce qui suit:

CHAPITRE I - DISPOSITIONS GENERALES

Article 1: Définitions

Aux fins de la présente Convention, on entend par:

a. "Paysage" : une portion de territoire, pouvant inclure les eaux côtières et/ou intérieures, telle qu'elle est perçue par les populations et dont l'aspect résulte de l'action de facteurs naturels et humains et de leurs interrelations;

b. "Protection paysagère" : les actions d'entretien des caractères existants d'un paysage, justifiées par sa valeur remarquable dérivant de sa configuration naturelle particulière ou du type d'intervention humaine le concernant;

c. "Gestion paysagère" : les actions visant, dans une perspective de développement durable, à assurer l'entretien régulier du paysage et à harmoniser ses évolutions induites par les nécessités économiques et sociales;

d. "Aménagement paysager" : les actions fondées sur des projets présentant un caractère prospectif particulièrement affirmé visant l'élaboration de nouveaux paysages en fonction des aspirations des populations concernées;

e. "Objectif de qualité paysagère" : la formulation par les autorités publiques compétentes des aspirations des populations en ce qui concerne les caractéristiques paysagères de leur cadre de vie.

Article 2 : Champ d'application

La présente convention s'applique à tout le territoire européen des Parties et porte sur les espaces naturels, ruraux, urbains et périurbains. Elle concerne aussi bien les paysages remarquables que les paysages ordinaires qui tous conditionnent la qualité du cadre de vie des populations en Europe.

Article 3 : Objectifs

Par la présente Convention chaque Partie s'engage à assurer la protection, la gestion et l'aménagement des paysages par la mise en place de mesures nationales et l'organisation d'une coopération européenne.

CHAPITRE II - MESURES NATIONALES

Article 4 : Répartition des compétences

Dans le cadre de son ordre juridique interne, chaque Partie détermine le meilleur niveau territorial de mise en oeuvre de la présente Convention selon la répartition des compétences qui lui est propre et dans le respect du principe de subsidiarité tel qu'il est défini par la Charte européenne de l'autonomie locale.

Article 5: General measures

Each Party undertakes:

a. to establish the legal principle that landscape is an essential component of the surroundings of human populations, an expression of the diversity of their shared cultural, ecological, social and economic heritage and the foundation of their identity;

b. to define and implement landscape policies aimed at landscape protection, management and planning through the adoption of the specific measures set out in Article 6 below;

c. to establish procedures for the participation of the general public, local and regional authorities and other parties interested in the definition and implementation of the landscape policies mentioned in paragraph b. above;

d. to accommodate landscape systematically in its town and country planning policies and in its cultural, environmental, agricultural, social and economic policies, as well as in any other sectoral policies with possible direct or indirect impact on landscape.

Article 6: Specific measures

I.   *Awareness-raising*

Each Party undertakes to conduct information and awareness-raising campaigns directed at public opinion, elected representatives and associations in order to arouse and increase awareness of the value of landscapes at present and in the future.

II. *Training and education*

Each Party undertakes:

a. to arrange training for specialists in landscape appraisal and operations;

b. to introduce multidisciplinary in-service training programmes for people in the various private- and public-sector occupational categories directly or indirectly concerned with landscapes;

c. to develop school and university courses which, in the relevant subject areas, address the values attaching to landscapes and the issues raised by their protection, management and planning.

III. *Identification and evaluation*

1. With the active participation of the interested parties, as stipulated in Article 5.c above, and with a view to

Article 5 : Mesures générales

Chaque Partie s'engage à:

a. consacrer juridiquement le paysage en tant que composante essentielle du cadre de vie des populations, expression de la diversité de leur patrimoine commun culturel, écologique, social et économique et fondement de leur l'identité;

b. formuler et à mettre en oeuvre des politiques paysagères visant la protection, la gestion et l'aménagement des paysages par l'adoption des mesures particulières visées à l'article 6 ci-dessous;

c. mettre en place des procédures de participation du public, des autorités locales et régionales et des autres acteurs concernés par la conception et la réalisation des politiques paysagères mentionnées à l'alinéa b. ci-dessus;

d. prendre en compte systématiquement le paysage dans leurs politiques en matière d'aménagement du territoire, d'urbanisme et dans leurs politiques culturelle, environnementale, agricole, sociale et économique ainsi que dans les autres politiques sectorielles pouvant avoir un effet direct ou indirect sur le paysage.

Article 6 : Mesures particulières

I.   *Sensibilisation*

Chaque Partie s'engage à entreprendre auprès de l'opinion publique, des élus et des associations, des campagnes d'information et de sensibilisation visant à éveiller et développer une conscience de la valeur des paysages présents et à venir.

II. *Formation et Education*

Chaque Partie s'engage à:

a. mettre en place la formation de spécialistes de la connaissance et de l'intervention sur les paysages;

b. instaurer des programmes pluridisciplinaires de formation continue pour les diverses catégories professionnelles privées et publiques concernées directement ou indirectement par le paysage;

c. développer des enseignements scolaire et universitaire abordant dans les disciplines intéressées, les valeurs attachées au paysage et les questions relatives à sa protection, sa gestion et son aménagement.

III. *Identification et évaluation*

1. En mobilisant les acteurs concernés conformément à l'article 5.c ci-dessus et en vue d'une meilleure connais-

improving knowledge of its landscapes, each Party undertakes:

a. to identify its own landscapes, including threatened landscapes, and to analyse their characteristics and the dynamics and pressures transforming them;

b. to determine the value of the landscapes thus identified, taking into account the particular values assigned to them by the interested parties.

2. These identification and evaluation procedures will gain from the exchanges of experience and methodology organised between Parties at European level pursuant to Article 8 of this convention.

IV.   *Landscape quality objectives*

Each Party undertakes to define landscape quality objectives for the landscapes identified and evaluated, doing so by means of a public consultation process at local level in accordance with Article 5.c above.

V.   *Procedures*

Taking into account the definition of landscape quality objectives, each Party undertakes to introduce procedures aimed at protecting, managing and/or planning landscape. These procedures may be based, for example, on those set out in the Appendix to this convention.

CHAPTER III - EUROPEAN CO-OPERATION

Article 7: Foundations

The Parties acknowledge that European landscapes constitute a common resource, for the protection, management and planning of which they have a duty to co-operate.

Article 8: Mutual assistance and exchange of information

The Parties undertake:

a. to render each other technical and scientific assistance in landscape matters through the pooling of experience and mutual disclosure of research projects;

b. to foster the exchange of landscape specialists in particular for training and information purposes;

c. to exchange information on all matters covered by the provisions of the convention.

Article 9: Transfrontier landscapes

The Parties undertake, wherever necessary, to set up international programmes for the protection, manage-

---

sance de son paysage, chaque Partie s'engage à:

a. identifier ses propres paysages, y compris les paysages menacés, à analyser leurs particularités ainsi que les dynamiques et les pressions qui les modifient;

b. évaluer les paysages identifiés en tenant compte des valeurs particulières qui leur sont attribuées par les acteurs concernés.

2. Les travaux d'identification et d'évaluation bénéficieront des échanges d'expériences et de méthodologies organisés entre les Parties à l'échelle européenne en application de l'article 8 de la présente Convention.

IV.   *Objectifs de qualité paysagère*

Chaque Partie s'engage à formuler des objectifs de qualité paysagère concernant les paysages identifiés et évalués, et ce, dans le cadre d'un processus de consultation publique à l'échelle locale, conformément à l'article 5.c ci-dessus.

V.   *Moyens d'intervention*

En tenant compte de la formulation des objectifs de qualité paysagère, chaque Partie s'engage à mettre en place des moyens d'intervention visant la protection, la gestion et/ou l'aménagement des paysages. Ces moyens pourront s'inspirer de ceux qui figurent, à titre d'exemple, en annexe à la présente Convention.

CHAPITRE III - COOPERATION EUROPEENNE

Article 7 : Fondements

Les Parties reconnaissent que les paysages européens constituent une ressource commune, pour la protection, la gestion et l'aménagement de laquelle ils ont le devoir de coopérer.

Article 8 : Assistance mutuelle et échange d'information

Les Parties s'engagent à:

a. se prêter une assistance technique et scientifique mutuelle par échange d'expériences et de travaux de recherche en matière de paysage;

b. favoriser les échanges de spécialistes du paysage notamment pour la formation et l'information;

c. échanger des informations sur toutes les questions visées par les dispositions de la présente Convention.

Article 9 : Paysages transfrontaliers

Les Parties s'engagent, en tant que de besoin, à préparer des programmes internationaux de protection, de gestion

ment and planning of transfrontier landscapes, in accordance with the provisions of this convention, relying as far as possible on local and regional authorities under the terms of the Outline Convention on Transfrontier Co-operation between Territorial Communities or Authorities in Europe.

Article 10: Implementation of the convention

1. The Committee of Ministers of the Council of Europe shall be responsible for promoting and monitoring the application of this convention. To this end, it may call upon the help of other Council of Europe bodies.

2. In accordance with paragraph 1 above, the Committee of Ministers shall be responsible in particular for:

a. making recommendations to the Parties concerning measures to be taken for the purposes of the convention, where necessary drawing their attention to threatened landscapes;

b. adopting guidelines for general and specific measures aimed at the protection, management or planning of national landscapes

c. promoting public awareness-raising and vocational training schemes and furthering exchanges of information and research findings in relation to landscapes, in accordance with Articles 6.I and 6.II of this convention;

d. encouraging programmes for the protection, management and planning of transfrontier landscapes in accordance with Article 9 of the convention;

e. awarding the "European Landscape Prize" and determining the criteria for so doing, in accordance with article 11 of the convention;

f. drawing up a "List of Landscapes of European Significance" and determining the criteria for inclusion in this list, in accordance with article 12 of the convention;

g. preparing a report every 5 years on the state and trends of the Parties' landscape policies and sending this report to the Parties and, for information, to the Parliamentary Assembly and the Congress of Local and Regional Authorities of Europe of the Council of Europe;

h. facilitating European co-operation in landscape matters particularly by such means as the raising from public and private bodies of voluntary financial contributions for the application of this convention, over and above the Parties' normal contributions;

i. preparing any necessary amendments to the convention and examining those proposed in accordance with Article 18 below.

et d'aménagement des paysages transfrontaliers conformément aux dispositions de la présente Convention en recourant, si possible, aux collectivités locales et régionales, sous les auspices de la Convention cadre européenne sur la coopération transfrontalière des collectivités ou autorités territoriales.

Article 10 : Mise en oeuvre de la Convention

1. Le Comité des Ministres du Conseil de l'Europe est chargé de promouvoir et suivre l'application de la présente Convention. Il peut à cet effet se faire assister par d'autres instances du Conseil de l'Europe.

2. En application du paragraphe 1 ci-dessus, Le Comité des Ministres est chargé en particulier:

a. de faire des recommandations aux Parties sur les mesures à prendre pour la mise en oeuvre de la Convention en attirant, si besoin est, l'attention des Parties sur les paysages menacés;

b. d'adopter des lignes directrices concernant les mesures générales et particulières visant la protection, la gestion ou l'aménagement des paysages nationaux;

c. de promouvoir des programmes de sensibilisation du public et de formation professionnelle et de favoriser l'échange d'informations et de recherches en matière de paysage conformément à l'article 6.I et 6.II ci-dessus;

d. d'encourager en application de l'article 9 de la présente Convention, des programmes de protection, de gestion et d'aménagement des paysages transfrontaliers;

e. d'attribuer le "Prix européen du paysage" et déterminer les critères de son attribution conformément à l'article 11 ci-dessous;

f. d'arrêter la "Liste des paysages d'intérêt européen" et déterminer les critères d'inscription sur celle-ci conformément à l'article 12 ci-dessous;

g. de préparer tous les 5 ans un rapport sur la situation et l'évolution des politiques paysagères des Parties et adresser ce rapport aux Parties et, pour information, à l'Assemblée parlementaire et au Congrès des pouvoirs locaux et régionaux de l'Europe du Conseil de l'Europe;

h. de faciliter la coopération européenne dans le domaine du paysage notamment en suscitant des contributions financières volontaires de la part d'organismes publics et privés pour l'application de la présente Convention s'ajoutant aux contributions normales des Parties;

i. de préparer les amendements nécessaires à la Convention et examiner ceux qui ont été proposés conformément à l'article 18. ci-après.

Article 11: European Landscape Prize

1. The "European Landscape Prize" is a distinction which may be conferred on local and regional authorities and their groupings that have instituted, as part of the landscape policy of a State party to this convention, a policy or measures to protect, manage and/or plan their landscape, which have proved lastingly effective and can thus serve as an example to other territorial authorities in Europe.

2. The Committee of Ministers shall define and publish the criteria on the basis of which it awards the "European Landscape Prize".

3. Applications for the "European Landscape Prize" shall be submitted to the Committee of Ministers by States. Transfrontier local and regional authorities may apply, as may groupings of local and regional authorities provided that they collectively manage the landscape in question.

4. The Committee of Ministers may award the "European Landscape Prize" to the territorial authorities selected, on the basis of an examination of applications submitted pursuant to paragraph 3 above and according to the criteria it has announced.

5. The award of the "European Landscape Prize" to local and regional authorities shall place them under an obligation to ensure the maintenance and lasting protection of the landscape areas concerned.

Article 12: List of Landscapes of European Significance

1. Any landscape of significance to all European populations may be registered on the "List of Landscapes of European Significance".

2. The Committee of Ministers shall define and publish the specific criteria on the basis of which a landscape may be registered on the "List of Landscapes of European Significance". These landscapes must already have been recognised as significant at national level;

3. Each Party to this convention may submit to the Committee of Ministers a request for landscapes in its territory to be registered on the "List of Landscapes of European Significance". Two or more Parties may submit a joint request concerning a transfrontier landscape.

4. Each request shall be accompanied by technical documentation identifying and evaluating the landscape in question and providing evidence of its European significance with regard to the specific criteria mentioned in paragraph 2 above.

5. On the basis of the requests submitted by the Parties in accordance with paragraph 3 above and with the criteria which it defines, the Committee of Ministers shall decide whether or not to register on the "List of Landscapes of

Article 11 : Prix européen du paysage

1. Peuvent se voir attribuer le "Prix européen du paysage" les collectivités locales et régionales et leurs groupements qui, dans le cadre de la politique paysagère d'un Etat Partie à la présente Convention, ont mis en place une politique ou des mesures visant la protection, le gestion et/ou l'aménagement de leurs paysages faisant la preuve d'une efficacité durable et pouvant ainsi servir d'exemple aux autres collectivités territoriales européennes.

2. Le Comité des Ministres définit et publie les critères sur la base desquels il attribue le "Prix européen du paysage".

3. Les demandes d'attribution du "Prix européen du paysage" seront transmises au Comité des Ministres par les Etats. Des collectivités locales et régionales transfrontalières peuvent être candidates ainsi que des regroupements de collectivités locales ou régionales à la condition qu'ils gèrent ensemble le paysage en question.

4. Sur la base de l'examen des demandes soumises en exécution du paragraphe 3. ci-dessus et des critères qu'il énonce, le Comité des Ministres peut attribuer aux collectivités territoriales sélectionnées le "Prix européen du paysage".

5. Le "Prix européen du paysage" impose aux collectivités locales et régionales qui en sont titulaires de veiller à la protection, la gestion et/ou l'aménagement durables des paysages concernés.

Article 12 : Liste des paysages d'intérêt européen

1. Peuvent être inscrits sur la "Liste des paysages d'intérêt européen" les paysages présentant un intérêt significatif pour l'ensemble des populations européennes.

2. Le Comité des Ministres définit et publie les critères particuliers sur la base desquels un paysage peut être inscrit sur la "Liste des paysages d'intérêt européen". Ces paysages doivent déjà avoir été reconnus pour leur intérêt significatif à l'échelle nationale.

3. Chacune des Parties peut soumettre au Comité des Ministres une demande d'inscription sur la "Liste des paysages d'intérêt européen" de paysages situés sur son territoire. Deux ou plusieurs Parties peuvent soumettre une demande conjointe en ce qui concerne un paysage transfrontalier.

4. Chaque demande doit être accompagnée d'une documentation technique identifiant et évaluant le paysage en question et justifiant de l'intérêt européen qu'il présente par rapport aux critères particuliers mentionnés au paragraphe 2 ci dessus.

5. Sur la base des demandes soumises par les Parties en exécution du paragraphe 3 ci-dessus et des critères qu'il énonce, le Comité des Ministres, décide ou non de l'inscription sur la "Liste des paysages d'intérêt européen" des

European Significance" landscapes within a country or astride a frontier after consulting the state or states concerned and, if appropriate, the interested local or regional authorities and non-governmental organisations. The registration shall be made only with the consent of the state(s) concerned.

6. The "List of Landscapes of European Significance" shall be regularly updated and published.

7. The Parties undertake to ensure the special protection of landscapes registered on the "List of Landscapes of European Significance", in accordance with the principles set forth in this convention and subject to a register of conditions compiled by the Committee of Ministers upon the registration of each landscape.

8. The Parties concerned by the registration shall submit a report to the Committee of Ministers every 3 years.

9. The Committee of Ministers, after hearing the Party(ies) concerned and consulting the local and regional authorities and associations concerned, may remove a landscape from the "List of Landscapes of European Significance" where the conditions mentioned in paragraph 7 above are not complied with and it no longer meets the criteria provided for in paragraph 2 above.

10. Inclusion in the "List of Landscapes of European Significance" may be independent of or additional to inclusion in the World Heritage List established pursuant to the UNESCO Convention for the Protection of the World Cultural and Natural Heritage.

11. Scientific co-operation and co-ordination between the UNESCO World Heritage Committee and the Committee of Ministers of the Council of Europe should be covered by an agreement between UNESCO and the Council of Europe, in accordance with Article 13.7 of the convention mentioned in paragraph 10 above.

12. The Committee of Ministers may instigate formal co-operation with other international organisations, non-governmental organisations and inter-governmental programmes involved in the protection, management and planning of the European landscape.

CHAPTER IV - FINAL CLAUSES

Article 13

The provisions of this convention shall not affect the application of more favourable specific provisions contained in other existing instruments of international law.

Article 14

1. This convention shall be open for signature by the member states of the Council of Europe. It shall be

---

paysages nationaux ou transfrontaliers concernés après consultation du ou des Etats impliqués ainsi que, le cas échéant, des autorités locales ou régionales et des organisations non gouvernementales intéressées. L'inscription ne peut se faire qu'avec le consentement de (ou des) l'Etat(s) intéressé(s).

6. La "Liste des paysages d'intérêt européen" fait l'objet d'une publication régulièrement mise à jour.

7. Les Parties s'engagent à spécialement protéger les paysages inscrits sur "Liste des paysages d'intérêt européen" conformément aux principes énoncés dans la présente Convention et en application d'un cahier des charges établi par le Comité des Ministres à l'occasion de chaque inscription.

8. Les Parties concernées par l'inscription sur la "Liste des paysages d'intérêt européen" présentent tous les 3 ans un rapport au Comité des Ministres.

9. Le Comité des Ministres peut, après audition de la (des) Partie(s) concernée(s) et consultation des autorités locales et régionales et des associations concernées, supprimer l'inscription d'un paysage de la "Liste des paysages d'intérêt européen" au cas où il ne respecterait pas le cahier des charges prévu au paragraphe 7 ci-dessus et ne correspondrait plus aux critères prévus au paragraphe 2 supra.

10. L'inscription sur la "Liste des paysages d'intérêt européen" peut être indépendante ou se cumuler avec l'inscription sur la Liste du patrimoine mondial arrêtée en application de la Convention de l'Unesco concernant la protection du patrimoine mondial culturel et naturel.

11. Une coopération scientifique et une coordination entre le Comité du patrimoine mondial de l'Unesco et le Comité des Ministres du Conseil de l'Europe devraient faire l'objet d'un accord entre l'Unesco et le Conseil de l'Europe en application de l'article 13.7 de la Convention mentionnée au paragraphe 10 ci-dessus.

12. Le Comité des Ministres peut susciter une coopération formelle avec les autres organisations internationales, les organisations non gouvernementales et les programmes intergouvernementaux concernés par la protection, la gestion et l'aménagement du paysage européen.

CHAPITRE IV - CLAUSES FINALES

Article 13

Les dispositions de la présente Convention ne portent pas atteinte à l'application des dispositions spécifiques plus favorables contenues dans d'autres instruments de droit international en vigueur.

Article 14

1. La présente convention est ouverte à la signature des Etats membres du Conseil de l'Europe. Elle sera soumise

subject to ratification, acceptance or approval. Instruments of ratification, acceptance or approval shall be deposited with the Secretary General of the Council of Europe.

2. The convention shall enter into force on the first day of the month following the expiry of a period of three months after the date on which three member states of the Council of Europe have expressed their consent to be bound by the convention in accordance with the provisions of the preceding paragraph.

3. In respect of any signatory states which subsequently express their consent to be bound by it, the convention shall enter into force on the first day of the month following the expiry of a period of three months after the date of the deposit of the instrument of ratification, acceptance or approval.

Article 15

1. After the entry into force of this convention, the Committee of Ministers of the Council of Europe may invite the European Community and any European State which is not a member of the Council of Europe, to accede to the convention by a majority decision as provided in Article 20 (d) of the Council of Europe Statute, and by the unanimous vote of the states Parties entitled to hold seats in the Committee of Ministers.

2. In respect of any acceding state, or the European Community in the event of its accession, the convention shall enter into force on the first day of the month following the expiry of a period of three months after the date of the deposit of the instrument of accession with the Secretary General of the Council of Europe.

Article 16

1. Any state may, at the time of signature or when depositing its instrument of ratification, acceptance, approval or accession, specify the territory or territories to which the convention shall apply, without limiting the scope stated in Article 2 above.

2. Any Contracting Party may at any later date, by declaration addressed to the Secretary General of the Council of Europe, extend the application of this convention to any other territory specified in the declaration. The convention shall take effect in respect of such a territory three months after the date of receipt of the declaration by the Secretary General.

3. Any declaration made under the two paragraphs above may, in respect of any territory mentioned in such declaration, be withdrawn by notification addressed to the Secretary General. Such withdrawal shall become effective on the first day of the month following the expiry of a period of three months after the date of receipt of the notification by the Secretary General.

à ratification, acceptation ou approbation. Les instruments de ratification, d'acceptation ou d'approbation seront déposés près le Secrétaire Général du Conseil de l'Europe.

2. La présente convention entrera en vigueur le premier jour du mois qui suit l'expiration d'une période de 3 mois après la date à laquelle trois Etats membres du Conseil de l'Europe auront exprimé leur consentements à être liés par la convention conformément aux dispositions du paragraphe précédent.

3. Pour tout signataire qui exprimera ultérieurement son consentement à être lié par la convention, celle-ci entrera en vigueur le premier jour du mois qui suit l'expiration d'une période de trois mois après la date du dépôt de l'instrument de ratification, d'acceptation ou d'approbation.

Article 15

1. Après l'entrée en vigueur de la présente convention, le Comité des Ministres du Conseil de l'Europe pourra inviter la Communauté Européenne et tout Etat européen non membre du Conseil de l'Europe à adhérer à la présente convention, par une décision prise à la majorité prévue à l'article 20 (d) du statut du Conseil de l'Europe, et à l'unanimité des Etats Parties ayant le droit de siéger au Comité des Ministres.

2. Pour tout Etat adhérent ou pour la Communauté Européenne en cas d'adhésion, la convention entrera en vigueur le 1er jour du mois qui suit l'expiration d'une période de trois mois après la date de dépôt de l'instrument d'adhésion près le Secrétaire Général du Conseil de l'Europe.

Article 16

1. Tout Etat peut au moment de la signature ou au moment du dépôt de son instrument de ratification, d'acceptation, d'approbation ou d'adhésion, désigner le ou les territoires auxquels s'appliquera la présente convention, sans pouvoir limiter le champ d'application visé à l'article 2 ci-dessus.

2. Toute Partie peut, à tout moment par la suite, par une déclaration adressée au Secrétaire Général du Conseil de l'Europe, étendre l'application de la présente convention à tout autre territoire désigné dans la déclaration. La convention entrera en vigueur à l'égard de ce territoire trois mois après la date de réception de la déclaration par le Secrétaire Général.

3. Toute déclaration faite en vertu des deux paragraphes précédents pourra être retirée en ce qui concerne tout territoire désigné dans cette déclaration, par notification adressée au Secrétaire Général. Le retrait prendra effet le premier jour du mois qui suit l'expiration d'une période de trois mois après la date de réception de la notification par le Secrétaire Général.

Article 17

1. Any Contracting Party may, at any time, denounce this convention by means of a notification addressed to the Secretary General of the Council of Europe.

2. Such denunciation shall become effective on the first day of the month following the expiry of a period of three months after the date of receipt of the notification by the Secretary General.

Article 18

1. Any Party may propose amendments to this convention.

2. Amendments shall be submitted in writing to the Secretary General of the Council of Europe and forwarded by him at least two months before the meeting of the Committee of Ministers to the member states of the Council of Europe and to any signatory state and Contracting Party.

3. The Committee of Ministers shall adopt any amendment by a three-quarters majority of votes cast. Any amendment shall be submitted to the Parties for acceptance.

4. Any amendment shall enter into force in respect of the Parties which have accepted it on the first day of the month following the expiry of a period of three months after the date on which three Council of Europe member states have informed the Secretary General of their acceptance. In respect of any Party which subsequently accepts it, such amendment shall enter into force on the first day of the month following the expiry of a period of three months after the date on which the said Party has informed the Secretary General of its acceptance.

Article 19

The Secretary General of the Council of Europe shall notify the member states of the Council of Europe, any signatory state having acceded to this convention and the European Community, if it accedes, of:

a. any signature;

b. the deposit of any instrument of ratification, acceptance, approval or accession;

c. any date of entry into force of this convention in accordance with Articles 14, 15, 16 and 18;

d. any report or decision established pursuant to Articles 10, 11 and 12;

e. any notification made under Article 17;

f. any other act, notification, information or communication relating to this convention.

In witness whereof the undersigned, being duly authorised thereto, have signed this convention.

Article 17

1. Toute Partie peut, à tout moment, dénoncer la présente convention en adressant une notification au Secrétaire Général du Conseil de l'Europe.

2. La dénonciation prendra effet le premier jour du mois qui suit l'expiration d'une période de trois mois après la date de réception de la notification par le Secrétaire Général.

Article 18

1. Toute Partie peut proposer des amendements à la présente convention.

2. Leur texte est soumis par écrit au Secrétaire Général du Conseil de l'Europe; il est transmis par ses soins à toute Partie contractante, à tout Etat signataire et aux Etats membres du Conseil de l'Europe.

3. Tout amendement est adopté par le Comité des Ministres à la majorité des trois quarts des voix exprimées. Il devra être soumis à l'acceptation des Parties.

4. Tout amendement entre en vigueur à l'égard des Parties qui l'ont accepté le premier jour du mois qui suit l'expiration d'une période de trois mois après la date à laquelle trois Parties membres du Conseil de l'Europe, auront informé le Secrétaire Général qu'elles l'ont accepté. Pour toute autre Partie qui l'aura accepté ultérieurement, l'amendement entrera en vigueur le premier jour du mois qui suit l'expiration d'une période d'un mois après la date à laquelle la dite Partie aura informé le Secrétaire Général de son acceptation.

Article 19

Le Secrétaire Général du Conseil de l'Europe notifiera aux Etats membres du Conseil de l'Europe, à tout Etat ayant adhéré à la présente convention et à la Communauté Européenne adhérente:

a. Toute signature;

b. Le dépôt de tout instrument de ratification, d'acceptation, d'approbation ou d'adhésion;

c. Toute date d'entrée en vigueur de la présente convention conformément aux articles 14, 15, 16 et 18;

d. Tout rapport et toute décision arrêtés en vertu des dispositions des articles 10, 11 et 12;

e. Toute notification faite en vertu de l'article 17;

f. Tout autre acte, notification, information ou communication ayant trait à la présente convention.

En foi de quoi, les soussignés dûment autorisés à cet effet, ont signé la présente Convention.

Done at ... , this ... , in English and French, both texts being equally authentic, in a single copy which shall be deposited in the archives of the Council of Europe. The Secretary General of the Council of Europe shall transmit certified copies to each member state of the Council of Europe and to any state or to the European Union should they be invited to accede to this convention.

Fait à ... le ... en français et en anglais, les deux textes faisant également foi, en un seul exemplaire qui sera déposé dans les archives du Conseil de l'Europe. Le Secrétaire Général du Conseil de l'Europe en communiquera copie certifiée conforme à chacun des Etats membres du Conseil de l'Europe ainsi qu'à tout Etat ou à la Communauté Européenne invités à adhérer à la présente Convention.

Appendix to the
Draft European Landscape Convention

Examples of specific legal, administrative, fiscal and financial measures for landscape protection, management and planning

Annexe au projet de
Convention européenne du paysage

Exemples de moyens juridiques, administratifs, fiscaux et financiers spécifiques qui peuvent être mis en place en vue de la protection, de la gestion et de l'aménagement des paysages

1. Drawing up long-range programmes or plans to determine the nature of the landscapes that will be passed on to future generations.

1. Elaboration de plans ou de programmes de longe durée visant à déterminer les caractères des paysages qui seront transmis aux générations futures.

2. Preparation of landscape plans at local or regional level, in particular for severely deteriorated or rapidly developing areas, including, where appropriate, the creation of new landscapes according to the aspirations of the populations concerned.

2. Elaboration de plans paysagers à l'échelle locale ou régionale notamment pour les zones particulièrement dégradées ou connaissant une évolution rapide prévoyant, le cas échéant, l'élaboration de nouveaux paysages en fonction des aspirations des populations concernées.

3. Consideration of landscape issues when programmes concerning protected natural areas and cultural sites are being defined and implemented.

3. Intégration des considérations paysagères dans le cadre de la conception et de la mise en oeuvre des programmes relatifs aux zones naturelles et aux sites culturels protégés.

4. Creation of a special status for landscapes that necessitate a specific protection measure or other type of action on account of their quality, rarity, historical and/or natural and/or other specific significance.

4. Edition d'un statut spécial pour les paysages dont la qualité, la rareté, l'intérêt historique et/ou naturel et/ou d'autres intérêts spécifiques, justifient une mesure particulière de protection ou un autre type d'action.

5. Inclusion of landscape aims and policies in existing town and country planning instruments at national, regional and local level, with particular emphasis on consideration of the landscape's value in building permit application files, and the inclusion of landscape considerations in environmental impact studies.

5. Intégration des objectifs et des politiques paysagers dans les instruments existants de planification de l'urbanisme et d'aménagement du territoire aux niveaux national, régional et local, y compris plus particulièrement la prise en compte de la valeur du paysage dans les dossiers de demande de permis de construire et inclusion des considérations paysagères dans le cadre des études d'impact sur l'environnement.

6. Accommodation of landscape quality objectives in major public works and infrastructure projects and in sectoral policies on the environment, agriculture, forestry, transport, social, cultural and industrial development and the future of the mining and tourist industries.

6. Intégration des objectifs de qualité paysagère dans la réalisation des grands ouvrages publics et des infrastructures ainsi que dans les politiques sectorielles en matière d'environnement, d'agriculture, de sylviculture, de transport, de développement social, culturel, industriel, minier et touristique.

7. Introduction of financial and/or fiscal incentives aimed at achieving more effective landscape protection, management or planning. Such measures should be adapted as far as possible to the different kinds of landscapes and to the needs of the local and regional authorities concerned.

7. Adoption de mesures d'incitation financière et/ou fiscale visant à assurer une protection, une gestion ou des aménagements paysagers plus efficaces. Ces mesures devront s'adapter le plus possible aux différents types de paysage et aux besoins des collectivités locales concernées.

8. Encouragement to all public or private bodies to draw up landscape protection, management and/or planning

8. Encouragement pour toute personne publique ou privée d'établir, avec des agriculteurs, des propriétaires

contracts with farmers, landowners or non-governmental organisations.

9. Injunctions to private owners of property in an area where the landscape has been identified and evaluated to take measures, in accordance with the landscape quality objectives previously defined, for the protection, management or planning of the landscape which is chiefly under their management.

10. Requests to public, semi-public and private bodies, including non-profit-making bodies, at national, regional and/or local level to take landscape protection, management or planning measures in respect of the areas which they own or manage, and to provide public access where appropriate.

11. In urgent cases, intervention by the responsible public authorities, which may delegate this task to non-governmental organisations concerned, in order to protect and safeguard exceptional or seriously threatened landscapes.

12. Where necessary and in cases where this constitutes the sole means of protecting a landscape, direct intervention by the public authorities in order to acquire a property on an amicable basis or by means of compulsory purchase with payment of due compensation.

fonciers ou des organisations non gouvernementales des contrats paysagers afin d'assurer la protection, de la gestion et/ou de l'aménagement des paysages.

9. Mise en demeure du propriétaire privé d'un bien faisant partie d'un zone dont le paysage a été préalablement identifié et évalué, de prendre des mesures de protection, de gestion ou d'aménagement du paysage dont il est le gestionnaire principal, conformément aux objectifs de qualité paysagère précédemment établis.

10. Demande aux organismes publics, semi-publics et privés, y compris ceux qui n'ont pas des buts lucratifs, aux niveaux national, régional et/ou local, d'adopter des mesures de protection, de gestion ou d'aménagement paysagers des espaces dont ils sont propriétaires ou gestionnaires ainsi que, le cas échéant, leur ouverture au public.

11. En cas d'urgence, intervention des autorités publiques responsables, pouvant déléguer cette tâche à des organisations non gouvernementales concernées, en vue de la protection des paysages exceptionnels ou gravement menacés afin de les sauvegarder.

12. En cas de besoin et dans le cas où cela constitue le seul moyen de protéger un paysage, intervention directe des autorités publiques pouvant prévoir l'acquisition amiable d'un bien ou son expropriation sur la base d'une indemnisation compensatrice.

ANNEX 1 B

Draft European Landscape Convention

Submitted to Select Committee of Experts on the Drafting of the European Landscape Convention, Strasbourg, 13 March 2000, Council of Europe, T-LAND (2000) 2 Revised 2

Projet de Convention européenne du paysage

Soumis au Comité restreint d'experts chargé de la rédaction de la Convention européenne du paysage, Strasbourg, le 3 mars 2000, Conseil de l'Europe, T-LAND (2000) 2 Révisé 2

PREAMBLE

The member States of the Council of Europe signatory hereto,

1. Considering that the aim of the Council of Europe is to achieve a greater unity between its members for the purpose of safeguarding and realising the ideals and principles which are their common heritage and that this aim is pursued in particular through agreements in the economic and social fields;

2. Concerned to achieve sustainable development based on a balanced and harmonious relationship between social needs, economic activity and the environment;

3. Noting that landscape, has an important public-interest role in the cultural, ecological, environmental and social fields and constitutes a resource favourable to economic activity and whose protection, management and planning can contribute to job creation;

4. Aware that landscape contributes to the formation of local cultures and that it is a basic component of the European natural and cultural heritage, contributing to human well-being and consolidation of the European identity;

5. Acknowledging that landscape is an important part of the quality of life for people everywhere: in in urban areas and in the countryside; in degraded areas as well as in areas of high quality; in areas recognised as outstanding as well as everyday areas;

6. Noting that developments in agriculture, forestry, industrial and mineral production techniques and in spatial planning, town planning, transport, infrastructure, tourism and recreation practices and, at a more general level, changes in the world economy are in many cases accelerating the transformation of landscapes;

7. Wishing to meet the desire of the public to play an active part in the development of landscapes and to enjoy high quality landscapes;

8. Believing that landscape is a key element of individual and social well-being and that its protection, management and planning entail rights and responsibilities for everyone;

9. Having regard to the legal texts existing at international level in the field of protection and management of the natural and cultural heritage, regional/spatial planning, local self-government and transfrontier co-operation, in particular the Convention on the Conservation of European Wildlife and Natural Habitats (Bern, 19 September 1979), the Convention for the Protection of the Architectural Heritage of Europe (Granada, 3 October 1985), the European Convention on the Protection of the Archaeological Heritage (revised) (Valletta, 16 January 1992), the European Outline Convention on Transfrontier Co-operation between Territorial Communities or Authori-

PREAMBULE

Les Etats membres du Conseil de l'Europe, signataires de la présente Convention,

1. Considérant que le but du Conseil de l'Europe est de réaliser une union plus étroite entre ses membres, afin de sauvegarder et promouvoir les idéaux et les principes qui sont leur patrimoine commun et que ce but est poursuivi en particulier par la conclusion d'accords dans les domaines économique et social;

2. Soucieux de parvenir à un développement durable fondé sur un équilibre harmonieux entre les besoins sociaux, l'économie et l'environnement;

3. Notant que le paysage participe de manière importante à l'intérêt général, sur les plans culturel, écologique, environnemental et social et qu'il constitue une ressource économique dont une gestion appropriée peut contribuer à la création d'emplois;

4. Conscients que le paysage concourt à l'élaboration des cultures locales et qu'il représente une composante fondamentale du patrimoine culturel et naturel de l'Europe, contribuant à l'épanouissement des êtres humains et à la consolidation de l'identité européenne;

5. Reconnaissant que le paysage est partout un élément important de la qualité de vie des populations : dans les milieux urbains et dans les campagnes, dans les territoires dégradés, comme dans ceux de grande qualité, dans les espaces remarquables comme dans ceux du quotidien;

6. Notant que les évolutions des techniques de production agricole, sylvicole, industrielle et minière et des pratiques en matière d'aménagement du territoire, d'urbanisme, de transport, de réseaux, de tourisme et de loisirs et, plus généralement, les changements économiques mondiaux continuent, dans beaucoup des cas, à accélérer la transformation des paysages;

7. Désirant répondre au souhait du public de jouir de paysages de qualité et de jouer un rôle actif dans leur transformation;

8. Persuadés que le paysage constitue un élément essentiel du bien-être individuel et social et que sa protection, sa gestion et son aménagement impliquent des droits et des responsabilités pour chacun;

9. Ayant à l'esprit les textes juridiques existant au niveau international dans les domaines de la protection et de la gestion du patrimoine naturel et culturel, de l'aménagement du territoire, de l'autonomie locale et de la coopération transfrontalière et notamment la Convention relative à la conservation de la vie sauvage et du milieu naturel de l'Europe (Berne, 19 septembre 1979), la Convention pour la sauvegarde du patrimoine architectural de l'Europe (Grenade, 3 octobre 1985), la Convention européenne pour la protection du patrimoine archéologique (révisée) (La Valette, 16 janvier 1992), la Convention cadre européenne sur la coopération transfrontalière des collectivi-

ties (Madrid, 21 May 1980), the European Charter of Local Self-government (Strasbourg, 15 October 1985), the Convention on Biological Diversity (Rio, 6 June 1992), the Convention concerning the Protection of the World Cultural and Natural Heritage (Paris, 16 November 1972); the Convention on Access to Information, Public Participation in Decision-making and Access to Justice on Environmental Matters (Aarhus, 25 June 1998);

10. Acknowledging that the quality and diversity of European landscapes constitute a common resource for the protection, management and planning of which Parties have a duty to co-operate;

11. Wishing to provide a new instrument devoted exclusively to the protection, management and planning of all types of landscapes in Europe;

Have agreed as follows:

CHAPTER I – GENERAL PROVISIONS

Article 1: Definitions

For the purposes of the Convention:

a. "Landscape" means an area, as perceived by people, whose character is the result of the action and interaction of natural and / or human factors;

b. "Landscape policy" means an expression by the competent public authorities of general principles, strategies and guidelines that permit the taking of specific measures aimed at the protection, management and planning of landscapes;

c. "Landscape quality objective" means, for a specific landscape, the formulation by the competent public authorities of the aspirations of populations with regard to the landscape features of their surroundings;

d. "Landscape protection" means action to conserve and maintain the significant or characteristic features of a landscape, justified by its heritage value derived from its natural configuration and/or from human activity;

e. "Landscape management" means action, from a perspective of sustainable development, to ensure the regular upkeep of a landscape, so as to guide and harmonise changes which are brought about by social, economic and environmental processes;

f. "Landscape planning" means forward-looking action to enhance, restore or create landscapes;

---

tés ou autorités territoriales (Madrid, 21 mai 1980), la Charte européenne de l'autonomie locale (Strasbourg, 15 octobre 1985), la Convention sur la diversité biologique (Rio, 6 juin 1992), la Convention pour la Protection du Patrimoine Mondial, Culturel et Naturel (Paris, 16 novembre 1972) ; Convention sur l'accès à l'information, la participation du public et l'accès à la justice dans le domaine de l'environnement (Aarhus, 25 juin 1998);

10. Reconnaissant que la qualité et la diversité des paysages européens constituent une ressource commune pour la protection, la gestion et l'aménagement de laquelle les Parties ont le devoir de coopérer;

11. Souhaitant instituer un instrument nouveau consacré exclusivement à la protection, à la gestion et à l'aménagement de tous les types de paysages européens;

Sont convenus de ce qui suit:

CHAPITRE I – DISPOSITIONS GÉNÉRALES

Article 1: Définitions

Aux fins de la présente Convention:

a. "Paysage" : désigne une partie de territoire telle que perçue par les populations, dont le caractère résulte de l'action de facteurs naturels et/ou humains et de leurs interrelations;

b. "Politique de paysage" : désigne la formulation par les autorités publiques compétentes des principes généraux, des stratégies et des orientations permettant l'adoption de mesures particulières en vue de la protection, la gestion et l'aménagement du paysage;

c. "Objectif de qualité paysagère" : désigne la formulation par les autorités publiques compétentes, pour un paysage donné, des aspirations des populations en ce qui concerne les caractéristiques paysagères de leur cadre de vie;

d. "Protection des paysages" : comprend les actions de conservation et de maintien des aspects significatifs ou caractéristiques d'un paysage, justifiées par sa valeur patrimoniale émanant de sa configuration naturelle, et/ou de l'intervention humaine;

e. "Gestion des paysages" : comprend les actions visant, dans une perspective de développement durable, à entretenir le paysage afin de guider et d'harmoniser les transformations induites par les évolutions sociales, économiques et environnementales;

f. "Aménagement des paysages" : comprend les actions présentant un caractère prospectif particulièrement affirmé visant la mise en valeur, la restauration ou la création de paysages.

Article 2: Scope

Subject to the provisions contained in Article 16 this Convention applies to the entire territory of the Parties and covers natural, rural, urban and peri-urban areas. It includes land, inland water and marine areas. It concerns landscapes that might be considered as everyday or degraded, as well as outstanding ones, since they all influence the quality of the surroundings in which people live.

Article 3: Aims

The aims of this Convention are to promote landscape protection, management and planning and to organise European co-operation on landscape issues.

CHAPTER II – NATIONAL MEASURES

Article 4: Division of responsibilities

Each Party shall implement this Convention, in particular Articles 5 and 6, according to its own division of powers, in conformity with its constitutional principles and administrative arrangements, and respecting the principle of subsidiarity, taking into account the European Charter of Local Self-government of 15 October 1985. [Each Party shall harmonise the implementation of this Convention with its own policies and programmes in a manner that meets the requirements of its own situation.]

Article 5: General measures

Each Party undertakes:

a. to recognise landscapes in law, as an essential component of people's surroundings, an expression of the diversity of their shared cultural and natural heritage and a foundation of their identity;

b. to establish and implement landscape policies aimed at landscape protection, management and planning through the adoption of the specific measures set out in Article 6 below;

c. to establish procedures for the participation of the general public, local and regional authorities and other parties with an interest in the definition and implementation of the landscape policies mentioned in paragraph b. above;

d. to integrate landscape into its spatial planning policies and in its cultural, environmental, agricultural, social and economic policies, as well as in any other policies with possible direct or indirect impact on landscape.

Article 2: Champ d'application

Sous réserve des dispositions de l'article 16, la présente Convention s'applique à tout le territoire des Parties et porte sur les espaces naturels, ruraux, urbains et périurbains. Elle inclut les espaces terrestres, les eaux intérieures et maritimes. Elle concerne tant les paysages qu'on pourrait considérer comme remarquables que les paysages dégradés, ou les paysages du quotidien qui, tous, conditionnent la qualité du cadre de vie des populations.

Article 3: Objectifs

La présente Convention a pour objet de promouvoir la protection, la gestion et l'aménagement des paysages et d'organiser la coopération européenne dans ce domaine.

CHAPITRE II – MESURES NATIONALES

Article 4: Répartition des compétences

Chaque Partie met en œuvre la présente Convention, et en particulier les articles 5 et 6, selon la répartition des compétences qui lui est propre, conformément à ses principes constitutionnels et à son organisation administrative et dans le respect du principe de subsidiarité, en tenant compte de la Charte européenne de l'autonomie locale du 15 octobre 1985. [Chaque Partie harmonise la mise en œuvre de la présente Convention avec ses propres politiques et programmes, de manière à satisfaire aux exigences de sa propre situation.]

Article 5: Mesures générales

Chaque Partie s'engage à:

a. reconnaître juridiquement le paysage en tant que composante essentielle du cadre de vie des populations, expression de la diversité de leur patrimoine commun culturel et naturel et fondement de leur identité ;

b. définir et à mettre en œuvre des politiques de paysage visant la protection, la gestion et l'aménagement des paysages par l'adoption des mesures particulières visées à l'article 6 ci-dessous;

c. mettre en place des procédures de participation du public, des autorités locales et régionales et des autres acteurs concernés par la conception et la réalisation des politiques de paysage mentionnées à l'alinéa b. ci-dessus;

d. intégrer le paysage dans leurs politiques d'aménagement du territoire, d'urbanisme et dans leurs politiques culturelle, environnementale, agricole, sociale et économique ainsi que dans les autres politiques pouvant avoir un effet direct ou indirect sur le paysage.

Article 6: Specific measures	**Article 6: Mesures particulières**
1. *Awareness-raising*	1. *Sensibilisation*
Each Party undertakes to increase awareness among the civil society, private organisations, and public authorities of the value of landscapes, their role and changes to them.	Chaque Partie s'engage à développer la sensibilisation de la société civile, des organisations privées et des autorités publiques à la valeur des paysages, leur rôle et leur transformation.
2. *Training and education*	2. *Formation et Education*
Each Party undertakes to promote:	Chaque Partie s'engage à promouvoir:
a. training for specialists in landscape appraisal and operations;	*a.* la formation de spécialistes de la connaissance et de l'intervention sur les paysages;
b. multidisciplinary training programmes in landscape policy, protection, management and planning for people in private and public and voluntary sector occupations directly or indirectly concerned with landscapes;	*b.* des programmes pluridisciplinaires de formation sur la politique, la protection, la gestion et l'aménagements des paysages destinés aux diverses professions du secteur privé et public et des associations concernées directement ou indirectement par le paysage;
c. school and university courses which, in the relevant subject areas, address the values attaching to landscapes and the issues raised by their protection, management and planning.	*c.* des enseignements scolaire et universitaire abordant dans les disciplines intéressées, les valeurs attachées au paysage et les questions relatives à sa protection, sa gestion et son aménagement.
3. *Identification and assessment*	3. *Identification et qualification*
a. With the active participation of the interested parties, as stipulated in Article 5.*c* above, and with a view to improving knowledge of its landscapes, each Party undertakes:	*a.* En mobilisant les acteurs concernés conformément à l'article 5.*c* ci-dessus et en vue d'une meilleure connaissance de ses paysages, chaque Partie s'engage à:

i.   – to identify its own landscapes throughout its territory
   – to analyse their characteristics and the forces and pressures transforming them
   – to take note of change;
	i. – identifier ses propres paysages, sur l'ensemble de son territoire
	   – à analyser leurs caractéristiques ainsi que les dynamiques et les pressions qui les modifient
	   – à en suivre les transformations;

ii. assess the landscapes thus identified, taking into account the particular values assigned to them by the interested parties and the population concerned.	*ii.* qualifier les paysages identifiés en tenant compte des valeurs particulières qui leur sont attribuées par les acteurs et les populations concernés.
b. These identification and assessment procedures shall be guided by the exchanges of experience and methodology organised between the Parties pursuant to Article 8 of this Convention.	*b.* Les travaux d'identification et de qualification seront guidés par des échanges d'expériences et de méthodologies organisés entre les Parties à l'échelle européenne en application de l'article 8 de la présente Convention.
4. *Landscape quality objectives*	4. *Objectifs de qualité paysagère*
Each Party undertakes to define landscape quality objectives for the landscapes identified and assessed after public consultation in accordance with Article 5.*c* above.	Chaque Partie s'engage à formuler des objectifs de qualité paysagère pour les paysages identifiés et après consultation du public, conformément à l'article 5.*c* ci-dessus.
5. *Implementation*	5. *Mise en œuvre*
To put landscape policies into effect, each Party undertakes to introduce instruments aimed at protecting, managing and/or planning landscape. These instruments may	Pour mettre en œuvre les politiques de paysage, chaque Partie s'engage à mettre en place des moyens d'intervention visant la protection, la gestion et/ou l'aménagement

be based, for example, on guidelines to be adopted by the European Landscape Committee pursuing Article 11 paragraph 1 b of this Convention.

CHAPTER III – EUROPEAN CO-OPERATION

Article 7: International Policies and Programmes

Parties undertake in co-operation to consider the landscape dimension of international policies and programmes and to recommend where relevant the inclusion in them of landscape considerations.

Article 8: Mutual assistance and exchange of information

In order to carry out the provisions of this Convention the Parties undertake to co-operate in order to enhance the effectiveness of measures taken under other articles of this Convention, and in particular:

a. to render each other technical and scientific assistance in landscape matters through the pooling of experience and mutual exchange of research projects;

b. to promote the exchange of landscape specialists in particular for training and information purposes;

c. to exchange information on all matters covered by the provisions of the Convention.

Article 9: Transfrontier landscapes

The Parties undertake, wherever necessary, to set up international programmes for the protection, management and planning of transfrontier landscapes, if necessary in collaboration with the local and regional authorities concerned.

Article 10: European Landscape Committee

1. For the purposes of this Convention, a European Landscape Committee shall be set up.

2. Each Party may be represented on the European Landscape Committee by one or more delegates. Each Party has the right to vote. Each State Party to this Convention shall have one vote. Concerning questions within its competence, the European Community shall exercise its right to vote and cast a number of votes equal to the number of Member States that are Parties to the Convention. The European Community shall not exercise its right to vote when the vote relates to a question, which does not fall within its competence.

The Parliamentary Assembly and the Congress of Local and Regional Authorities of Europe of the Council of Europe may be represented on the European Landscape Committee by one or more delegates, without the right to vote.

des paysages. Ces moyens pourront s'inspirer, par exemple, des lignes directrices qui seront adoptées par le Comité européen du paysage conformément à l'article 11.*b* de la présente Convention.

CHAPITRE III – COOPÉRATION EUROPÉENNE

Article 7: Politiques et programmes internationaux

Les Parties s'engagent à coopérer lors de la prise en compte de la dimension paysagère dans les politiques et programmes internationaux et à recommander le cas échéant que les considérations concernant le paysage y soient incorporées.

Article 8: Assistance mutuelle et échange d'information

Pour l'exécution des dispositions de la présente Convention, les Parties s'engagent à coopérer pour renforcer l'efficacité des mesures prises conformément aux articles de la présente Convention, et en particulier:

a. se prêter une assistance technique et scientifique mutuelle par échange d'expériences et de travaux de recherche en matière de paysage;

b. favoriser les échanges de spécialistes du paysage notamment pour la formation et l'information;

c. échanger des informations sur toutes les questions visées par les dispositions de la présente Convention.

Article 9: Paysages transfrontaliers

Les Parties s'engagent, en tant que de besoin, à préparer des programmes internationaux de protection, de gestion et d'aménagement des paysages transfrontaliers en y associant, les cas échéant, les collectivités locales et régionales concernées.

Article 10: Comité européen du paysage

1. Il est constitué, aux fins de la présente Convention, un Comité européen du Paysage.

2. Chaque Partie peut se faire représenter au sein du Comité européen du paysage par un ou plusieurs délégués. Chaque Partie dispose d'un droit de vote. Chaque Etat Partie à la présente Convention a une voix. Sur les questions relevant de sa compétence, la Communauté européenne exerce son droit de vote et exprime un nombre de voix égal au nombre de ses Etats membres qui sont Parties à la Convention. La Communauté européenne ne vote pas lorsque le vote porte sur une question qui ne relève pas de sa compétence.

L'Assemblée parlementaire et le Congrès des pouvoirs locaux et régionaux de l'Europe du Conseil de l'Europe peuvent se faire représenter au Comité européen du paysage par un ou plusieurs délégués, sans droit de vote.

3. Any member State of the Council of Europe or the European Community, which is not a Party to the Convention, may be represented on the European Landscape Committee by an observer.

The European Landscape Committee may, by unanimous decision, invite any non-member State of the Council of Europe, which is not a Party to the Convention to be represented by an observer at one of its meetings.

The European Landscape Committee may, on its own initiative or at the request of the body or agency concerned, invite any body or agency technically qualified in the protection, management or planning of landscapes to be represented by an observer at all or part of one of its meetings.

4. The European Landscape Committee shall be convened by the Secretary General of the Council of Europe. Its first meeting shall be held within one year of the date of the entry into force of the Convention. It shall subsequently meet at least every four years and whenever a majority of the Parties so request.

5. In order to discharge its functions, the European Landscape Committee may, on its own initiative, set up an Executive Group whose members will represent equitably the main regions and cultures of Europe, and arrange for meetings of groups of experts.

6. A majority of the Parties shall constitute a quorum for holding a meeting of the European Landscape Committee.

7. Subject to the provisions of this Convention, the European Landscape Committee shall draw up at its first meeting its own Rules of Procedure, including the conditions for admission of observers.

Article 11: Responsibilities of the European Landscape Committee

1. The European Landscape Committee shall be responsible for overseeing the application of this Convention.

It may in particular:

a. make recommendations to the Parties concerning measures to be taken for the purposes of the Convention, where necessary drawing their attention to threatened landscapes;

b. adopt guidelines for general and specific measures aimed at the protection, management or planning of landscapes and commend them to Parties;

c. encourage public awareness-raising, vocational training schemes and encourage exchanges of information and research findings in relation to landscapes, in accordance with Articles 6 paragraph 1 and 6 paragraph 2 of this Convention;

3. Tout Etat membre du Conseil de l'Europe ou la Communauté européenne, qui n'est pas Partie à la présente Convention, peut se faire représenter au Comité européen du paysage par un observateur.

Le Comité européen du paysage peut, à l'unanimité, inviter tout Etat non-membre du Conseil de l'Europe qui n'est pas Partie à la Convention à se faire représenter par un observateur à l'une de ses réunions.

Le Comité européen du Paysage peut, de sa propre initiative ou à la demande de l'organisme ou de l'institution concernée, inviter tout organisme ou toute institution techniquement qualifié dans le domaine de la protection, de la gestion et de l'aménagement du paysage à être représenté(e) par un observateur à tout ou partie d'une de ses réunions.

4. Le Comité européen du paysage est convoqué par le Secrétaire Général du Conseil de l'Europe. Il tient sa première réunion dans le délai d'un an à compter de la date d'entrée en vigueur de la Convention. Il se réunit par la suite au moins tous les quatre ans et, en outre, lorsque la majorité des Parties en formule la demande.

5. Pour s'acquitter de ses fonctions, le Comité européen du paysage peut, de sa propre initiative, établir un Comité exécutif, dont les membres devront représenter équitablement les principales régions et cultures de l'Europe et instituer des réunions de groupes d'experts.

6. La majorité des Parties constitue le quorum nécessaire pour tenir une réunion du Comité européen du paysage.

7. Sous réserve des dispositions de la présente Convention, le Comité européen du paysage établit à sa première réunion son règlement intérieur y compris les conditions d'admission des observateurs.

Article 11: Responsabilités du Comité européen du paysage

1. Le Comité européen du paysage est chargé de veiller à l'application de la présente Convention.

Il peut en particulier:

a. faire des recommandations aux Parties sur les mesures à prendre pour la mise en œuvre de la Convention en attirant, si besoin est, l'attention des Parties sur les paysages menacés;

b. adopter des lignes directrices concernant les mesures générales et particulières visant la protection, la gestion ou l'aménagement des paysages et les transmettre aux Parties;

c. encourager des programmes de sensibilisation du public et de formation professionnelle et favoriser l'échange d'informations et de recherches en matière de paysage conformément à l'article 6 paragraphe 1 et 6 paragraphe 2 de la présente Convention;

d. encourage programmes for the protection, management and planning of transfrontier landscapes in accordance with Article 9 of the Convention;

e. determine the criteria for the award of the "European Landscape Award" and recommend the award, in accordance with article 12 of the Convention.

f. consider the desirability of establishing a means of European recognition for landscapes which form a component of the common heritage and the diverse cultural identities of the people of Europe, on the basis that

    i. criteria for such recognition are prepared and published by the European Landscape Committee,

    ii. such landscapes are identified and proposed by the States Parties to the Convention;

g. prepare regular reports on the progress in the implementation of the Convention and send these reports to the Parties and, for information, to the Committee of Ministers, to the Parliamentary Assembly and the Congress of Local and Regional Authorities of Europe and other relevant Committees of the Council of Europe;

h. facilitate European co-operation in landscape matters particularly by such means as the raising from public and private bodies of voluntary financial contributions for the application of this Convention;

i. prepare any necessary amendments to the Convention and examine those proposed in accordance with Article 18 of this Convention.

j. make any proposal for improving the effectiveness of this Convention.

2. The European Landscape Committee shall use its best endeavours to facilitate a friendly settlement of any difficulty to which the execution of this Convention may give rise.

3. After each meeting, the European Landscape Committee shall forward to the Committee of Ministers of the Council of Europe a report on its work and on the operation on the Convention.

Article 12: European Landscape Award

1. The "European Landscape Award" is a distinction which may be conferred by the Council of Europe on local and regional authorities and their groupings that have instituted, as part of the landscape policy of a Party to this Convention, a policy or measures to protect, manage and/or plan their landscape, which have proved lastingly effective and can thus serve as an example to other territorial authorities in Europe. The distinction may be also conferred on non-governmental organisa-

d. encourager en application de l'article 9 de la présente Convention, des programmes de protection, de gestion et d'aménagement des paysages transfrontaliers;

e. déterminer les critères d'attribution du "Prix européen du paysage" et recommander son octroi, conformément à l'article 12 de la présente Convention;

f. considérer l'opportunité d'établir un moyen de reconnaissance au niveau européen des paysages formant une composante du patrimoine commun et la diversité des identités culturelles des populations européennes avec pour fondement que:

    i. les critères d'une telle reconnaissance sont formulés et publiés par le Comité européen du paysage,

    ii. ces paysages sont identifiés et proposés par les Etats parties à la Convention;

g. préparer des rapports périodiques sur le progrès dans la mise en œuvre de la convention et adresser ces rapports aux Parties et, pour information au Comité des Ministres, à l'Assemblée parlementaire et au Congrès des pouvoirs locaux et régionaux de l'Europe, ainsi qu'à d'autres comités appropriés du Conseil de l'Europe;

h. faciliter la coopération européenne dans le domaine du paysage notamment en suscitant des contributions financières volontaires de la part d'organismes publics et privés pour l'application de la présente Convention;

i. préparer les amendements nécessaires à la Convention et examiner ceux qui ont été proposés conformément à l'article 18 de la présente Convention.

j. faire toute proposition tendant à améliorer l'efficacité de la Convention.

2. Le Comité européen du paysage facilite autant que de besoin le règlement amiable de toute difficulté rencontrée dans l'exécution de la Convention.

3. Après chacune de ses réunions, le Comité européen du paysage transmet au Comité des Ministres du Conseil de l'Europe un rapport sur ses travaux et sur le fonctionnement de la Convention.

Article 12: Prix européen du paysage

1. Peuvent se voir attribuer par le Conseil de l'Europe le "Prix européen du paysage" les collectivités locales et régionales et, leurs groupements qui, dans le cadre de la politique de paysage d'une Partie à la présente Convention, ont mis en œuvre une politique ou des mesures visant la protection, la gestion et/ou l'aménagement durable de leurs paysages faisant la preuve d'une efficacité pérenne et pouvant ainsi servir d'exemple aux autres collectivités territoriales européennes. La distinction

tions or individuals having made particularly remarkable contributions to landscape protection, management or planning.

2. The European Landscape Committee shall define the criteria on the basis of which to recommend the award of the "European Landscape Award", adopt its rules and publicise the Award.

3. Applications for the "European Landscape Award" shall be submitted to the Secretary General of the Council of Europe by States. Transfrontier local and regional authorities, and appropriate non-governmental organisations or individuals may apply, as may groupings of local and regional authorities provided that they jointly manage the landscape in question.

4. On proposals from the European Landscape Committee the Committee of Ministers of the Council of Europe shall award the "European Landscape Award" to the territorial authorities, organisations or individuals selected, on the basis of an examination of applications submitted pursuant to paragraph 3 above and according to the rules of the Award.

5. The award of the "European Landscape Award" to local and regional authorities shall place them under an obligation to ensure the lasting protection, management and/or planning of the landscape areas concerned.

CHAPTER IV – FINAL CLAUSES

Article 13: Relationship with other instruments

The provisions of this Convention shall not prejudice stricter provisions concerning landscape protection, management and planning contained in other existing or future binding national or international instruments.

Article 14: Signature, ratification and entry into force

1. This Convention shall be open for signature by the member states of the Council of Europe. It shall be subject to ratification, acceptance or approval. Instruments of ratification, acceptance or approval shall be deposited with the Secretary General of the Council of Europe.

2. The Convention shall enter into force on the first day of the month following the expiry of a period of three months after the date on which five member states of the Council of Europe have expressed their consent to be bound by the Convention in accordance with the provisions of the preceding paragraph.

3. In respect of any signatory state which subsequently expresses its consent to be bound by it, the Convention shall enter into force on the first day of the month following the expiry of a period of three months after the

pourra également être attribuée aux organisations non gouvernementales ou à des individus qui ont fait preuve d'une contribution particulièrement remarquable à la protection, la gestion ou l'aménagement du paysage.

2. Le Comité européen du paysage définit et publie les critères sur la base desquels il recommande l'attribution du "Prix européen du paysage", adopte son règlement et fait connaître le prix.

3. Les candidatures du "Prix européen du paysage" seront transmises au Comité européen du paysage par les Etats. Des collectivités locales et régionales transfrontalières ainsi que et les organisations non gouvernementales et des individus appropriés peuvent être candidates ainsi que des regroupements de collectivités locales ou régionales à la condition qu'ils gèrent ensemble le paysage en question.

4. Sur propositions du Comité européen du paysage, le Comité des Ministres du Conseil de l'Europe attribue le "Prix européen du paysage" aux collectivités territoriales, organisations ou individus sélectionnés sur la base de l'examen des candidatures soumises selon le paragraphe 3 ci-dessus et selon le règlement du prix.

5. Le "Prix européen du paysage" impose aux collectivités locales et régionales qui en sont titulaires de veiller à la protection, la gestion et/ou l'aménagement durables des paysages concernés.

CHAPITRE IV – CLAUSES FINALES

Article 13: Relations avec d'autres instruments

Les dispositions de la présente Convention ne portent pas atteinte aux dispositions plus strictes en matière de protection, de gestion ou d'aménagement des paysages contenues dans d'autres instruments nationaux ou internationaux contraignants qui sont ou entreront en vigueur.

Article 14: Signature, ratification, entrée en vigueur

1. La présente Convention est ouverte à la signature des Etats membres du Conseil de l'Europe. Elle sera soumise à ratification, acceptation ou approbation. Les instruments de ratification, d'acceptation ou d'approbation seront déposés près le Secrétaire Général du Conseil de l'Europe.

2. La présente Convention entrera en vigueur le premier jour du mois qui suit l'expiration d'une période de trois mois après la date à laquelle cinq Etats membres du Conseil de l'Europe auront exprimé leur consentements à être liés par la Convention conformément aux dispositions du paragraphe précédent.

3. Pour tout signataire qui exprimera ultérieurement son consentement à être lié par la Convention, celle-ci entrera en vigueur le premier jour du mois qui suit l'expiration d'une période de trois mois après la date du dépôt de

date of the deposit of the instrument of ratification, acceptance or approval.

l'instrument de ratification, d'acceptation ou d'approbation.

Article 15: Accession

1. After the entry into force of this Convention, the Committee of Ministers of the Council of Europe may invite the European Community and any European State which is not a member of the Council of Europe, to accede to the Convention by a majority decision as provided in Article 20 (d) of the Council of Europe Statute, and by the unanimous vote of the states Parties entitled to hold seats in the Committee of Ministers.

2. In respect of any acceding state, or the European Community in the event of its accession, the Convention shall enter into force on the first day of the month following the expiry of a period of three months after the date of the deposit of the instrument of accession with the Secretary General of the Council of Europe.

Article 16: Territorial Application

1. Any state or the European Community may, at the time of signature or when depositing its instrument of ratification, acceptance, approval or accession, specify the territory or territories to which the Convention shall apply.

2. Any Party may at any later date, by declaration addressed to the Secretary General of the Council of Europe, extend the application of this Convention to any other territory specified in the declaration. The Convention shall take effect in respect of such a territory on the first day following the expiry of a period of three months after the date of receipt of the declaration by the Secretary General.

3. Any declaration made under the two paragraphs above may, in respect of any territory mentioned in such declaration, be withdrawn by notification addressed to the Secretary General. Such withdrawal shall become effective on the first day of the month following the expiry of a period of three months after the date of receipt of the notification by the Secretary General.

Article 17: Denunciation

1. Any Party may, at any time, denounce this Convention by means of a notification addressed to the Secretary General of the Council of Europe.

2. Such denunciation shall become effective on the first day of the month following the expiry of a period of three months after the date of receipt of the notification by the Secretary General.

Article 18: Amendments

1. Any Party or the European Landscape Committee may propose amendments to this Convention.

Article 15: Adhésion

1. Après l'entrée en vigueur de la présente Convention, le Comité des Ministres du Conseil de l'Europe pourra inviter la Communauté européenne et tout Etat européen non membre du Conseil de l'Europe à adhérer à la présente Convention, par une décision prise à la majorité prévue à l'article 20 (d) du statut du Conseil de l'Europe, et à l'unanimité des Etats Parties ayant le droit de siéger au Comité des Ministres.

2. Pour tout Etat adhérent ou pour la Communauté européenne en cas d'adhésion, la Convention entrera en vigueur le 1er jour du mois qui suit l'expiration d'une période de trois mois après la date de dépôt de l'instrument d'adhésion près le Secrétaire Général du Conseil de l'Europe.

Article 16: Application territoriale

1. Tout Etat ou la Communauté européenne peut au moment de la signature ou au moment du dépôt de son instrument de ratification, d'acceptation, d'approbation ou d'adhésion, désigner le ou les territoires auxquels s'appliquera la présente Convention.

2. Toute Partie peut, à tout moment par la suite, par une déclaration adressée au Secrétaire Général du Conseil de l'Europe, étendre l'application de la présente Convention à tout autre territoire désigné dans la déclaration. La Convention entrera en vigueur à l'égard de ce territoire le premier jour du mois qui suit l'expiration d'une période de trois mois après la date de réception de la déclaration par le Secrétaire Général.

3. Toute déclaration faite en vertu des deux paragraphes précédents pourra être retirée en ce qui concerne tout territoire désigné dans cette déclaration, par notification adressée au Secrétaire Général. Le retrait prendra effet le premier jour du mois qui suit l'expiration d'une période de trois mois après la date de réception de la notification par le Secrétaire Général.

Article 17: Dénonciation

1. Toute Partie peut, à tout moment, dénoncer la présente Convention en adressant une notification au Secrétaire Général du Conseil de l'Europe.

2. La dénonciation prendra effet le premier jour du mois qui suit l'expiration d'une période de trois mois après la date de réception de la notification par le Secrétaire Général.

Article 18: Amendements

1. Toute Partie ou le Comité européen du paysage peut proposer des amendements à la présente Convention.

2. Any proposal for amendment shall be notified to the Secretary General of the Council of Europe who shall communicate it to the member States of the Council of Europe, to the other States party, and to any non-member State which has been invited to accede to this Convention in accordance with the provisions of Article 15. The Secretary General of the Council of Europe shall convene a meeting of the European Landscape Committee at the earliest two months after the communication of the proposal.

3. The European Landscape Committee shall examine any amendment proposed and submit the text adopted by a majority of three quarters of the members of the European Landscape Committee to the Committee of Ministers for approval. Following its adoption by the Committee of Ministers by the majority provided for in Article 20.d of the Statute of the Council of Europe and by the unanimous vote of the States Parties entitled to hold seats in the Committee of Ministers, the text shall be forwarded to the Parties for acceptance.

4. Any amendment shall enter into force in respect of the Parties which have accepted it on the first day of the month following the expiry of a period of three months after the date on which three Council of Europe member states have informed the Secretary General of their acceptance. In respect of any Party which subsequently accepts it, such amendment shall enter into force on the first day of the month following the expiry of a period of three months after the date on which the said Party has informed the Secretary General of its acceptance.

Article 19: Notifications

The Secretary General of the Council of Europe shall notify the member states of the Council of Europe, any signatory state and the European Community having acceded to this Convention, of:

a. any signature;

b. the deposit of any instrument of ratification, acceptance, approval or accession;

c. any date of entry into force of this Convention in accordance with Articles 14 , 15 and 16;

d. any declaration made under Article 16;

e. any proposal for amendment, any amendment adopted pursuant to Article 18 and the date on which it comes into force;

f. any denunciation made under Article 17;

g. any other act, notification, information or communication relating to this Convention.

In witness whereof the undersigned, being duly authorised thereto, have signed this Convention.

Done at ..., this ..., in English and French, both texts being equally authentic, in a single copy which shall be deposited in the archives of the Council of Europe. The Secretary General of the Council of Europe shall transmit certified copies to each member state of the Council of Europe and to any state or to the European Community should they be invited to accede to this Convention.

Fait à ... le ... en français et en anglais, les deux textes faisant également foi, en un seul exemplaire qui sera déposé dans les archives du Conseil de l'Europe. Le Secrétaire Général du Conseil de l'Europe en communiquera copie certifiée conforme à chacun des Etats membres du Conseil de l'Europe ainsi qu'à tout Etat ou à la Communauté européenne invités à adhérer à la présente Convention.

Appendix

Annexe

Terms of reference of the Select Committee of Experts on the drafting of the European Landscape Convention

Mandat du Comité restreint d'experts chargé de la rédaction de la Convention européenne du paysage

1. Name of committee

1. Nom du Comité

Select Committee of Experts on the Drafting of the European Landscape Convention.

Comité restreint d'experts chargé de la rédaction de la Convention européenne du paysage.

2. Type of committee

2. Type de Comité

Select Committee of Experts.

Comité restreint d'experts.

3. Source of terms of reference

3. Source du mandat

Committee of Ministers.

Comité des Ministres.

4. Terms of reference

4. Mandat

To finalise the text of a European Landscape Convention on the basis of the Draft European Landscape Convention prepared by the Congress of Local and Regional Authorities of Europe (CLRAE). Particular attention will be paid to Articles 12 and 10 (body to follow the implementation of the Convention).

Finaliser le texte d'une Convention européenne du paysage sur la base du projet de Convention européenne du paysage préparé par le Congrès des pouvoirs locaux et régionaux de l'Europe (CPLRE). Une attention particulière sera accordée à l'article 12 et à l'article 10 (organe chargé de suivre la mise en œuvre de la Convention).

5. Membership of the committee

5. Composition du Comité

–   Twelve members (six appointed by CO-DBP from its members and six appointed by CC-PAT from its members).

–   Douze membres (six nommés par CO-DBP parmi ses membres et six nommés par le CC-PAT parmi ses membres).

–   The Council of Europe will bear (from the budgets allocated to the Directorates of Environment and Local Authorities and of Education, Culture and Sport for the intergovernmental programmes of activity for 1999 and 2000) the travel and subsistence costs of the experts.

–   Le Conseil de l'Europe prend à sa charge (sur les budgets attribués pour les Programmes intergouvernementaux d'activités 1999 et 2000 aux Directions de l'Environnement et des Pouvoirs locaux, et de l'Enseignement, de la Culture et des Sports) les frais de voyage et de séjour des experts.

–   The CLRAE and the Parliamentary Assembly may participate in meetings without the right to vote or to have expenses refunded.

–   Le CPLRE et l'Assemblée parlementaire peuvent participer aux réunions sans droit de vote, les frais étant à la charge des budgets de ces organes.

–   The European Commission may participate in meetings without the right to vote or to have expenses refunded.

–   La Commission européenne peut participer aux réunions sans droit de vote et sans droit de remboursement des frais de participation.

–   Any other country will be able to participate in the work undertaken as observer.

–   Tout autre pays pourra participer aux travaux menés à titre d'observateur.

6.   Structures and working methods

– The Committee shall meet at most three times.

– The Committee will submit to the Committee of Ministers, through the CO-DBP and the CC-PAT, a text of a European Landscape Convention with a view to its adoption and opening for signature.

7.   Duration

The terms of reference expire on 28 February 2000.

6.   Structure et méthode de travail

– Le Comité se réunira un maximum de trois fois.

– Le Comité transmettra au Comité des Ministres par le biais du CO-DBP et du CC-PAT, un texte d'une Convention européenne du paysage en vue de son adoption et ouverture à la signature.

7.   Durée

Le mandat expire le 28 février 2000.

ANNEX 2

Pan-European Biological and Landscape Diversity Strategy
Action Theme 4: Conservation of Landscape

Council of Europe, UNEP, European Centre for Nature Conservation, 1996

Paneuropéenne de la Diversité Biologique et Paysagère Stratégie
Domaine d'action n°4: Conservation des paysages

Conseil de l'Europe, PNUE, Centre européen pour la conservation de la nature, 1996

Challenges to be addressed:

To prevent further deterioration of the landscapes and their associated cultural and geological heritage in Europe, and to preserve their beauty and identity. To correct the lack of integrated perception of landscapes as a unique mosaic of cultural, natural and geological features and to establish a better public and policy maker awareness and more suitable protection status for these features throughout Europe.

Opportunities to be considered:

Cultural and social commitment to maintaining local and regional individuality as expressed by cultural and geological heritage features in the landscape. Opportunities abound to restore many of these features such as traditional field and landscape patterns, using existing policy and measures. Public and private landowner participation and partnerships offer immediate opportunities to ensure conservation of landscapes, cultural and geological heritage. Treaty of Maastricht (Articles 92(3) and 128) Council of Europe Draft Recommendation on the Integrated Conservation of Cultural Landscape Areas as part of Landscape Policies, Council of Europe Draft Landstape Charter. European Convention on Archaeological Heritage, European Convention on Architectural Heritage, Mediterranean Landscape Charter, IUCN Parks for Life: Action for Protected Areas in Europe, National town and country planning mechanisms, Digne Declaration (ProGeo).

Focus on Pan-European objectives:

4.1   Compile a comprehensive reference guide on European biological and landscape diversity to further develop and seek acceptance of criteria to identify priorities for conserving geological and cultural landscape features, and list threatened landscapes and geological sites of Pan-European significance and identify most suitable mechanisms for their conservation; identify traditional agricultural and related landscape management types, and assess the effect of marginalization or intensification ort the landscape (1996-1997).

4.2   Establish guidelines following assessment and evaluation to address policies, programmes and legislation for the protection of cultural heritage, of geological heritage and of biological diversity that are mutually supportive and complementary, and use them to their full

Les défis à relever:

Enrayer la dégradation des paysages en Europe et du patrimoine culturel et géologique qu'ils représentent. Préserver leur beauté et leur identité. Faire en sorte, ce qui n'est pas le cas actuellement, que l'on ait une vision d'ensemble des paysages et qu'on les envisage comme constituant une mosaïque unique de caractéristiques culturelles, naturelles et géologiques; faire en sorte également que le public et la classe politique soient davantage sensibilisés et que les paysages soient mieux protégés dans toute l'Europe.

Les textes et les moyens à employer:

S'engager, d'un point de vue culturel et social, à préserver l'individualité locale et régionale telle qu'elle s'exprime à travers les caractéristiques du patrimoine culturel et géologique que sont les paysages. Il existe de multiples possibilités de restaurer, par le biais des politiques et des mesures existantes, un grand nombre de ces caractéristiques, comme les champs et les paysages traditionnels. La participation du public et des propriétaires privés et les partenariats que l'on peut établir avec eux constituent autant d'occasions immédiates d'oeuvrer à la conservation des paysages, ainsi que du patrimoine culturel et géologique. On pourra se fonder également sur le Traité de Maastricht (Articles 92 (3) et 128), le projet de Recommandation du Conseil de l'Europe sur la conservation intégrée des paysages culturels dans le cadre des politiques paysagères, le projet de Charte du paysage du Conseil de l'Europe, la Convention européenne pour la protection du patrimoine archéologique, la Convention pour la sauvegarde du patrimoine architectural du Conseil de l'Europe, la Charte du paysage méditerranéen. L'initiative Parks for Life: Action Plan for protected areas in Europe de l'UICN, les outils d'aménagement du territoire, la Déclaration de Digne (ProGeo).

Les objectifs paneuropéens:

4.1   Constituer un guide de référence exhaustif sur la diversité biologique et paysagère européenne afin de préciser et faire accepter les critères qui devront présider à la conservation des caractéristiques paysagères géologiques et culturelles; recenser les paysages et sites géologiques d'importance paneuropéenne qui sont menacés; définir les mécanismes les plus aptes à assurer leur conservation; définir les modes traditionnels d'agriculture et de gestion du paysage; évaluer les effets de la marginalisation des terres ou de l'intensification des modes d'exploitation agricole sur le paysage (1996-1997).

4.2   Puis, au terme de cette évaluation, dresser une liste de lignes directrices relatives aux politiques, aux programmes et aux législations complémentaires et se renforçant mutuellement, de nature à assurer la protection du patrimoine culturel, du patrimoine géologique et de la

potential in the conservation of the landscape (1996-2000). Particular emphasis will be to review options to:

- Encourage countries to adopt and implement initiatives under the Council of Europe Draft Recommendation of the Council of Ministers to Member States on the Integrated Conservation of Cultural Landscape Areas as part of Landscape Policies (CDCC-BU(95) 7) (1996-1998).

- Develop mechanisms to promote involvement of existing international protected area processes in Europe, including World Heritage Sites, Biosphere Reserves and European Diploma Sites, in the conservation of landscapes and geological features (1996-2000).

4.3   Set up a Code of Practice to involve private and public landowners to promote awareness of the relevance for biodiversity of landscapes traditionally valued and managed for their historical and cultural importance, focusing on historic parkland estates and historic buildings (1996-1998).

4.4   Establish an action plan using awareness techniques, guidelines and demonstration models to safeguard geological features in the landscape, actively involve and consult landowners and the energy, industry and water management sectors in their conservation (1996-1998).

4.5   Investigate the relationship between traditional landscape and regional economy. Develop a framework to stimulate initiatives for regional development based on landscape diversity, involving eco-tourism and traditional crafts. Find successful case studies and set up programmes for exchange of expertise (1996-2000).

diversité biologique; faire en sorte d'exploiter toutes les possibilités en matière de conservation du paysage (1996-2000). On mettra l'accent en particulier sur les différentes options qui existent pour:

- Encourager les pays à adopter et à mettre en oeuvre des initiatives dans le cadre du projet de Recommandation du Comité des Ministres du Conseil de l'Europe destinée à promouvoir la conservation des zones du paysage culturel dans le cadre des politiques paysagères (CDCC-BU(95) 7) (1996-1998).

- Elaborer des mécanismes susceptibles de promouvoir la contribution des dispositifs internationaux existant en matière d'aires protégées en Europe, dont les Sites du patrimoine mondial, les Réserves de la Biosphère et les Sites diplômés européens, à la conservation des paysages et des caractéristiques géologiques (1996-2000).

4.3   Elaborer un Code de conduite afin que les propriétaires publics ou privés contribuent, eux aussi, à faire comprendre le rôle de la biodiversité des paysages traditionnellement appréciés et gérés pour leur importance historique et culturelle, en mettant l'accent sur les domaines boisés et sur les bâtiments historiques (1996-1998).

4.4   Dresser un plan d'action en utilisant des techniques de sensibilisation, des lignes directrices et des modèles de démonstration pour sauvegarder les caractéristiques géologiques du paysage, donner aux propriétaires et aux secteurs de l'énergie, de l'industrie et de la gestion de l'eau la possibilité de prendre une part active à leur conservation (1996-1998).

4.5   Etudier en profondeur les relations qui existent entre paysage traditionnel et économie régionale. Mettre en place un cadre de travail qui permettra de stimuler les initiatives en faveur d'un développement régional guidé par la nécessité de préserver la diversité paysagère, comme celles qui concernent l'écotourisme et les arts et métiers traditionnels. Trouver des exemples d'études de cas réussies et mettre en place des programmes d'échanges d'information entre spécialistes (1996-2000).